Southern Living. GARDEN G

Perennials

Series Editor: Lois Trigg Chaplin

Oxmoor House®

Contents

©1996 by Oxmoor House, Inc.
Book Division of Southern Progress Corporation
P.O. Box 2463, Birmingham, Alabama 35201

Southern Living® is a federally registered
trademark of Southern Living, Inc.

Library of Congress Catalog Number: 95-74603
ISBN: 0-8487-2241-8
Manufactured in the United States of America
Fourth Printing 1998

Editor-in-Chief: Nancy Fitzpatrick Wyatt
Editorial Director, Special Interest Publications:
Ann H. Harvey
Senior Editor, Editorial Services: Olivia Kindig Wells
Art Director: James Boone

Southern Living Garden Guide PERENNIALS

Series Editor: Lois Trigg Chaplin
Assistant Editor: Kelly Hooper Troiano
Copy Editor: Jennifer K. Mathews
Editorial Assistant: Laura A. Fredericks
Garden Editor, *Southern Living*: Linda C. Askey
Indexer: Katharine R. Wiencke
Concept Designer: Eleanor Cameron
Designer: Carol Loria
Senior Photographer, *Southern Living*: Van Chaplin
Production and Distribution Director: Phillip Lee
Associate Production Managers: Theresa L. Beste,
Vanessa D. Cobbs
Production Coordinator: Marianne Jordan Wilson
Production Assistant: Valerie L. Heard

Our appreciation to the staff of *Southern Living*
magazine for their contributions to this book.

Japanese roof iris

Cannas

Cover: *Coneflowers*
Frontispiece: *Daylilies*

Swamp sunflower, Mexican bush sage

Perennials Primer

The golden blooms of perennial coreopsis contrast vividly with the short-lived mealycup sage.

Perennials are constants in the garden, adding color and life for several seasons.

Perennials bring repeated color, fragrance, and texture to your garden through the seasons, year after year. Compared to annuals, which live a year or less, perennials are more permanent components of your garden that will last for several years. Most perennials have fleshy stems and foliage that are killed by cold or put to rest by summer heat, but their roots survive. These plants wax and wane on a seasonal clock, repeating the cycle for many years.

Perennials are not easily categorized, but you will find that most fit one or more of the following descriptions. *Half-hardy* perennials, such as azure sage, are perennial only in areas with mild winters; elsewhere they are grown as annuals. *Ephemeral* perennials may live a long time, but their blooms and foliage last only a short while each year. A good example is Virginia bluebells, which come up, bloom, and disappear within three months. Quite the opposite are *evergreen* perennials, such as hellebores and dianthus, which keep their leaves year-round and often serve as ground covers.

A few perennials are *shrubby,* developing woody shrublike stems; an example is tree peony. These perennials usually need pruning to keep them vigorous and full. *Short-lived* perennials can be enjoyed for just two or three years and then must be replaced. Finally, *long-lived* perennials live for many years, some for decades. Peonies, among the most durable, may outlive the gardener.

Because perennials live for years, multiplying and spreading, you will probably share them by giving away pieces or divisions or by digging them up entirely. Iris, daisies, and mums are but a few of the dozens of perennials that tend to multiply.

Unlike shrubs, which grow larger each year and eventually become too bulky to transplant, perennials are always easily moved (although a few may resent it), allowing you the freedom to rearrange and replace them. This means you may be tempted to transplant them to a spot where they look better, smell stronger, or appear brighter in combination with another plant. In fact, the fun of growing perennials is finding just the right spot where a plant looks best and then deciding which other plants should accompany it.

No matter which selections you choose, these pages will give you information and ideas for enjoying perennials in your garden.

Sedum Autumn Joy is one of the most popular fall-flowering perennials because it goes through many interesting changes of form and color from spring until winter.

The lingering blooms of summer (lantana, pentas, cosmos, and Mexican heather) merge with the new blossoms of fall-blooming Mexican bush sage.

Perennials in the Landscape

Integrate perennials into the landscape to bring new color to the green of trees and shrubs. These beds border a sidewalk and are sure to make visitors slow down as they approach the front door.

The flowers and foliage of perennials offer a smorgasbord of color and texture for all seasons.

Using perennials in the landscape is one of the most rewarding aspects of gardening as perennials have the quality that gardeners value most—color. Like the use of color indoors, placing color in the garden with perennial plants requires careful planning and involves inevitable trial and error; you may often find yourself digging up and moving plants to a better location. Because perennials are so varied, their uses will range from the simplicity of a single clump in a pot to the formality of a full-blown English-style border—or to whatever artistic placement you decide to try.

Refer to these pages for ideas for placing perennials in your garden, both in relation to each other and to other types of plants. Also, study the photographs for the suggestions they make.

Spots of Color in the Garden

Use perennials as spots of color in places where you want to attract a visitor's eye. They may mark the entrance to your home, the foot of a fountain or a birdbath, a patio cutout, or any other carefully identified space. Spots of color call for perennials that look good for the longest possible time, such as Goldsturm coneflower, yarrow, showy sedum, salvia, and coreopsis. Do not plant perennials to "hide" an air-conditioning unit or other eyesore; flowers simply draw more attention to it.

Small Flower Beds

Often we think of perennials in only one form—a large border. However, the majority of perennials are not displayed in a border, serving instead as plants in a small flower bed. This is especially effective when perennials are paired with annuals that fill the void when the perennials are not in bloom. Small flower beds may be placed in the corner of a landscape, sandwiched between a walkway and a wall, or located beside a patio or in a courtyard. When planning a small bed, it is critical to choose perennials that look good for a long time. If the bed is in a prominent spot, provide them with some evergreen accompaniment, such as a small shrub.

Coneflowers offer a spot of color in a green garden whose show otherwise depends on the contrast of leaf textures.

Clumps of Japanese roof iris, white bearded iris, and pink peony are all that are needed in this small flower bed. After the blooms fade, the foliage will remain handsome for months.

A classic border often follows a color theme, such as that of pastels. However, the look of the border will change from season to season as the various perennials reach their seasonal peaks and then give way to other plants.

Large Borders

Large perennial beds and the mix of perennials within them define a classic English treatment called a border. A border always needs to have a good background to help the plants stand out. Typically a border is planted with a color theme, such as pastel, all white, or bright colors. Plants chosen are those with as much seasonal variety as possible so that the border offers color from the very earliest to the very latest possibility of bloom. Annuals, which bloom for months, are often used to fill color gaps between the waxing and waning of perennials, ensuring the border always has something to offer.

To allow plenty of room for combining perennials successfully, your border should be at least 6 feet deep; 10 feet is better, and it may, of course, be as long as your space, time, and money allow. The classic border treatment also involves a fair amount of shoveling, as you are rarely entirely satisfied with the initial placement of plants.

Ground Covers

A few perennials are sturdy enough to be used as ground covers. Many of these will spread to blanket the ground with handsome evergreen foliage so that the plants look good even when not in bloom. Evergreen daylilies and hellebores are excellent choices. However, perennials used in this manner require a bit more maintenance than typical ground covers in that they may need to be divided to rejuvenate the planting.

Woodland Gardens

Perennials can bring color to even the shadiest settings. Many of the perennials suited to a woodland garden are native wildflowers. They can carpet the periphery of a walkway or enliven the large, mulched shady areas of suburban lots. Perennials such as hellebore, a classic for shade, also make sturdy evergreen ground covers that bring winter color to wooded settings.

Hostas and ajuga make a handsome ground cover.

Butterfly and Hummingbird Gardens

You can create a feeding ground for butterflies and hummingbirds by selecting perennials that are attractive to these creatures. The larger the garden, the more effective it will be. This garden will demand full sun and should include bright red, orange, and yellow blooms. To be especially attractive to butterflies, your garden should include plants on which they lay their eggs, such as butterfly weed and parsley.

Color in Containers

Growing perennials in pots allows you to put the color right where you want it on a patio, a deck, or a porch. Good perennials for pots are evergreens, such as Bath's Pink, or plants that put on a display for many weeks, such as showy sedum.

The butterfly garden at the Biltmore House in Asheville, North Carolina, is typical of this type of garden, with its bright-colored plants that attract both butterflies and hummingbirds.

You can also plan a succession of potted perennials year-round by choosing several that bloom in different seasons and planting them in small plastic containers. When one plant is in bloom, slip the plastic pot into a decorative clay one; replace with another perennial when the show has faded.

You may mix perennials in a large pot to provide a variety of color and form. Pair upright plants, such as iris, with cascading ones, such as candytuft. It is best to choose evergreen perennials with contrasting foliage so they will look good when not in bloom.

Goldenrod and aster are only two of many perennials that are grown for flower arranging.

Perennials for a Cutting Garden

The ideal way to grow flowers for cutting is to disregard clashing colors and plant heights. The most practical cutting garden has its own space set apart from the landscape and is planted in rows rather than groups of similar color and size. This permits you to replace plants as they wane without upsetting the layout and allows extra spacing between plants so that the flowers can grow large and their stems strong. Plants crammed close together in a flower border are not the best flowers for cutting because crowding makes the stems thin and weak.

Blue phlox and bearded iris are a good pair of spring perennials that complement each other in both color and form.

PRACTICAL POINTERS

• Put the tallest plants toward the back of a bed, or plant them in the center of a bed that will be viewed from all sides.

• Remember plant compatibility. What makes the plants you choose grow best: sun or shade, wet or dry soil? Do not mix plants with opposite needs or your bed will have a ragged appearance as one plant thrives and another struggles.

• When mixing perennials with other plants, do not plant just one unless it is a very large plant, such as Mexican bush sage. Instead, plant in trios or fives. Place plants so that they form an equilateral triangle or a sweep. They will grow together to make one clump, which will have more visual impact than a single plant.

• When planning a large flower bed, remember that it will look more lush and full if you design it to be viewed down its length.

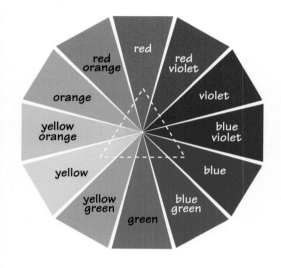

Colors and Combinations

You will enjoy your garden most when you use flowers and foliage to paint a picture that changes with the seasons. Translating a rainbow of flowers into an orchestrated design calls for a careful study of the perennials available to you. Investigate color and texture combinations as if you were decorating a room. With a little planning you can take advantage of the vast array of perennials that may be used in nearly every garden.

Start with the Color Wheel

While selecting color is a matter of personal taste, the color wheel on this page shows how colors naturally work together. The wheel is an artist's tool for previewing the impact of certain color combinations; it also helps simplify color selection. To use this color wheel, cut a small equilateral triangle of paper and position it on the wheel so that its points are on the three primary colors—red, yellow, and blue. As you rotate the triangle, the points indicate trios of complementary colors that work well together, making it easy for you to group flowers of corresponding colors.

Also consider the color of your home and the surrounding areas when planning your garden. For instance, red brick does not make a good backdrop for red flowers, but red blooms are exquisite against a gray wall or sidewalk. Here are some considerations for employing the colors of perennials in your landscape design.

Using Color in the Garden

• Start with green. For a successful foreground of perennial flowers and colorful foliage, you need a background, and often the best is a wall of leafy green. Evergreen shrubs are especially nice during the winter months because they provide constant foliage while the bed is otherwise dormant.

A dark background provides perennials and other flowers a surface against which to stand out. Here, coreopsis is accompanied by the globes of allium (a bulb) in front of a hedge.

Blues and lavenders can be used to unify a border of flowers of various shades.

• Use blue liberally for various effects. You can create excitement by pairing color-wheel opposites, such as blue and orange or yellow. For a quieter mood, combine blue with white, pale pink, silver, or violet; these shades emphasize the coolness of blue.

• Punctuate with color. The use of color for bold accents is limited only by your imagination. Consider a spot of strong color near an entryway to define it and attract attention; if you have a primarily evergreen garden, use color in pots or beds to enliven the green. You may also use color to punctuate a flower border by choosing a shade that is particularly vibrant or contrasts well with the surrounding flowers.

• Use color to impart mood. Warm colors—red, orange, and bright yellow—attract attention by suggesting both sunshine and flame. They make a garden happy and lively and can also make it warm and cozy. Such colors become good choices for the winter and early spring garden but are perhaps less appealing for summer, when you do not need to add warmth. In contrast, white, blue, and pastel flowers seem cooler and are pleasant choices for a tree-shaded spot in the summertime. Soft, quiet colors are often preferred for formal gardens where evergreens such as boxwoods and a sculpture, a topiary, or a water feature are the main attraction.

QUESTIONS TO ASK WHEN SELECTING PERENNIALS

To combine plants that will complement each other, you should know as much about each plant as possible. Here are some questions to ask that will help you pair plants with compatible growth, form, bloom times, and horticultural requirements.

How tall and wide will it grow?
When does it bloom?
Does it like sun or shade?
Does it spread?
What shape and color are the
    flowers?
How long does it bloom?
Does the foliage stay green
    through winter?
Will it tolerate poor soil or bad
    drainage?
Does it form clumps?
Does it reseed?

• Use color to control space. Warm-colored blooms attract your eye and stand out against the background. They are more noticeable, tending to come forward in the landscape, thereby shrinking the space between the plant and your eye. Warm-colored blooms can make a large garden feel smaller and more intimate. On the other hand, the cool colors—especially blue and violet—tend to recede, so cool-colored blooms appear minimized and make a small space seem larger.

• Use color to unify. Repeating one shade of blooms, such as white, will bring unity to an assortment of colored flowers.

• Use white for nighttime enjoyment. White is both striking and clearly visible under moonlight or outdoor lighting. The most effective white flowers are flat blooms, such as those of single peonies. Light-colored foliage, such as the large leaves of chartreuse hostas, also show up well after dark. Because nighttime is often the only opportunity you have to enjoy a deck or patio, always consider such plants for at least one spot in your garden.

The repetition of colors and plants creates harmony. Pansies in yellow and blue along with pink geraniums fill in between perennial candytuft, peonies, and iris.

Perennials with Attractive Foliage

Some perennials, such as lamb's-ear and hosta, are more prized for their foliage than for their flowers, due to the colors and textures of their leaves. These perennials can lift a bed from ordinary to extraordinary by giving the viewer a surprise. Just when you expect flowers, leaves instead create the show, such as the visual excitement produced by the vivid contrast of chartreuse hosta foliage with deep-colored ground covers, such as purple ajuga.

The silver foliage of lamb's-ear is every bit as showy as a flower, if not more so. The fuzzy, silvery-white leaves beckon from a distance and shimmer in both sunlight and moonlight. You can use silver to enhance any color, as it provides a gentle backdrop to the richness of annuals such as purple globe amaranth or orange marigolds and perennials pale or bright. Place silver foliage behind a green-leafed plant, such as the fan-shaped bearded iris, to create a stunning silhouette. Like white flowers, silver foliage is more prominent than green at night.

A perennial with variegated foliage becomes an accent when surrounded by darker leaves or the leafy woodland floor. It may also enliven any nearby flowers with its contrasting colors. Use the colors of the foliage of annuals, shrubs, and other perennials to enhance the show.

Hosta provides excellent textural contrast with surrounding plants, such as English ivy, sweet woodruff, another hosta, and acanthus.

Foliage color and texture can be as important as flower color in a combination. Here the purple leaves of Setcreasea purpurea *repeat the color of Japanese iris. The composition is sparked by yellow coreopsis (right) and yarrow (left) with white calla lily peeping through.*

15

Perennials in the Landscape

This spring array in shades of pink, purple, and white includes iris, daisies, chives, petunias, sweet William, and pansies.

A small monument is the focus of this summer garden of lamb's-ear and yellow yarrow.

PLANTINGS FOR EACH SEASON

Planning around the seasons is the key to keeping yearlong perennial color in your garden. These photographs show some colorful examples. The reward comes in mixing perennials with annuals and shrubs that overlap the seasons, filling the gaps between blooms.

This fall garden includes
chrysanthemums, showy
sedum, coneflowers,
salvia, and the annual
narrowleaf zinnia.

Bearsfoot hellebore is
unique in that it provides
flowers and evergreen
foliage in winter.

Getting Started

Starting with healthy plants and the knowledge of how to handle them is critical to your success.

Perennial transplants, or seeds for starting your own, are often obtained from mail-order sources, which offer a wide choice of selections.

The most difficult part of growing perennials is getting started. It takes thoughtful planning and the wise investment of time and money to select plants, prepare the soil, and properly plant perennials that will reward you for years to come.

Consumer Horticulture

When you visit the garden center or order perennials from a mail-order source, be familiar with the form in which the plant is sold. Perennials are likely to be either in containers or *bare root,* that is, without soil on their roots. Prepare the soil properly, provide good drainage, and plant right away.

Potted Perennials

Perennials grown in containers are young plants that are ready to be planted directly in the garden. The most economical way to purchase them is as transplants in *cell packs* (three, four, or six units grouped together, each containing one plant). A few perennials, such as evergreen candytuft, dianthus, and Shasta daisies, are sometimes sold in these smaller packs; however, most perennials come in larger pots because they live for a long time and are likely to remain in the pot for a while. Some of the gallon-sized plants may be a year old when you buy them; the larger size of these plants is an advantage if you plant late in the growing season.

Here are a few tips to help you buy potted perennials for mass planting, typically those that will be used to carpet the ground. Four-inch pots come 16 to a flat, with one plant per pot. You will find many of the best buys in 4-inch pots, as the plants are generally large enough for good growth the first season and cost less than 1-gallon plants.

Bare-Root Plants

You will seldom find bare-root perennials at garden centers, but many that you order through mail-order sources will be shipped this way. Bare-root plants should be packed in moist peat moss or sawdust so that their roots remain moist. Plant soon after they arrive, first soaking the roots for a few hours.

Select Healthy Plants

Check plants for signs of insects or disease. If the foliage appears mottled, look at the underside of the leaves for aphids, whiteflies, or spider mites. If the plants appear weak, slip one out of the container to check the roots. Healthy roots are white and fibrous; soft or brown roots are a sign of disease. It is also crucial that you purchase plants that have been properly cared for. Those that spend days baking in a sidewalk display and are allowed to severely wilt between waterings will not grow into healthy plants.

Buy Fresh Seed

To save money, you may start a few perennials, such as evergreen candytuft, from seed, either in the garden or indoors. (Turn to page 30 for more about starting seeds indoors.) Just remember that starting from seed is more economical than buying transplants only if done correctly. Always buy seed that is dated for the current year and only purchase packets that have been properly stored in a cool, dry environment. Seed in packets that are wrinkled with moisture or left sitting in the sun may have lost viability.

Storing Transplants and Seed

When you cannot plant everything the day you bring it home, make sure you keep the plants and seed in top condition until you can get them in the ground. Place transplants outdoors in partial shade, with protection from afternoon sun, and water daily. If they sit for more than two weeks, water with a diluted liquid fertilizer. Try not to wait more than a week or two or the plants can quickly become rootbound and stunted. Store unused seed in a sealed plastic container in the refrigerator or freezer. Never leave it in an outdoor storage room or anywhere it might be exposed to water or humidity. Bare-root plants may be stored in their packaging in the crisper drawer of the refrigerator for a few days.

Breaking Ground

The perennials you plant are only as good as the conditions you provide for them. Granted, some plants tolerate neglect better than others, but all do best with some basic care. If you give them the right amount of sunlight, good soil, and proper watering and feeding, they will grow larger and bear more flowers than poorly tended plants.

Preparing the Planting Bed

The ideal soil is loose enough to allow roots to easily expand and is porous, well drained, and able to retain moisture and nutrients. But such soil is rarely found naturally around your home. You must

HINTS FOR BREAKING NEW GROUND

• When testing your soil, take samples from different parts of the area to get an accurate reading.

• Mark the outline of a new bed by stretching a garden hose out in the shape of the bed, or draw the proposed edges with spray paint. The lines will help you keep your weed killer within bounds.

• Never work the soil when it is wet, as it will dry in clods. However, tilling is easier if the soil is slightly moist, especially heavy clay soil. Water the day before tilling, or plan your project to follow a light rain.

Spread a layer of organic matter over the bed before setting plants. This is also a good time to add lime, if needed, and starter fertilizer.

create your own by adding wheelbarrow loads of organic matter, such as compost, manure, or sphagnum peat moss. Organic matter improves clay soil by opening it up so that roots can properly breathe and drain. On the other hand, it helps poor, sandy soil hold more moisture and nutrients.

When possible, begin preparing your soil a few weeks before planting so that you can do the job in stages rather than all at once. If the spot has never been cultivated, begin by removing anything growing there. You can transplant healthy grass to bare spots elsewhere in the yard or spray the entire area with a nonselective herbicide to kill existing grass and weeds. (Remember that these products will kill every green thing that they touch, so follow label directions carefully.) Once in the ground, these substances decompose to nitrogen, water, phosphate, and carbon dioxide. In a week to 10 days you can break up the dead vegetation with a turning fork or tiller and remove it to a compost pile.

Use a turning fork or tiller to work the soil as deeply as possible, preferably 12 to 18 inches in heavy clay. Never work wet soil as it will dry in clods. Spread a layer of organic matter 3 to 4 inches deep over the area and work this with your fork until well blended with your native soil. Each time you work organic matter into the soil it becomes softer, making your work easier. The first time is always the most difficult.

Till the bed to incorporate the organic matter, fertilizer, and lime (if needed) at least 8 inches into the soil.

If you need to add lime to reduce the soil acidity (raise the pH), do so as soon as possible. Often the most practical time to add lime is when you first till the bed. However, it takes weeks for pulverized lime to raise the soil pH, so you may want to use hydrated lime, which acts more quickly. This type is also more caustic, so follow label precautions carefully.

Good Drainage Is Essential

The most common cause of problems with perennials is a poorly drained planting site. There are a few perennials, such as cannas, that do not mind soggy soil, but most need good drainage to avoid root rot. If you cannot plant on a site that drains well, build a raised bed for your plants.

Always Do a Soil Test

You may have trouble assessing your soil's chemistry. Is the soil acidity too high or low? How much nitrogen, phosphorus, and potassium does it need? In certain areas of the country, salt levels are high; in others, the native soil may be deficient in a crucial element. A soil test will tell you what your soil needs.

Soil test kits are available through your county Agricultural Extension service office. The kit contains directions for testing, along with a form to record your findings. Most states charge a small fee, but it is worth the cost to determine exactly what your soil requires for healthy plants.

A raised bed is essential to the health of perennials in soils that do not drain well. Poor drainage will cause plants to decline or rot.

ABOUT RAISED BEDS

You can raise the level of the soil to improve drainage by building a bed on top of the ground. Till the native soil as if preparing it for planting. This helps the soil in the raised area drain into the ground below.

There are endless ways to build a raised bed, ranging from simply mounding the soil about a foot high to building a box from landscape timbers, mortared brick, or stacked stone. When filling the raised bed, be sure to incorporate native soil along with compost in the soil mix. (Do not include native soil if you have had problems with plants rotting at the base or roots, or if plants have been stunted by nematodes.)

Planting

Proper planting is essential to the success of your perennials. Their health and vigor will be best if they get a good start, which includes everything from the way the young plants are handled to the soil in which they grow.

Arrange your perennials before planting to give you a glimpse of how they will look next to each other. By doing this before digging, you will be able to make changes more easily.

Handling Perennials in Containers

Keep plants in containers watered and in shade until you are ready to plant. Ideally, you should plant right away. Never let them sit around for more than two weeks.

Remove a transplant from its pot by turning the pot upside down and sliding the plant out. Never grab the stem and pull it or you may tear it from its roots. Remember, young plants need to be handled gently.

Plants that have been growing in their pots for a while may have become rootbound. That is, their roots may have formed an impenetrable mat and may be growing out the holes at the bottom of the container. In this case, you should carefully break up the mat to encourage the roots to grow. For perennials with large roots, such as hostas and daylilies, you can simply take your finger and pull the roots away from the tangled mass. However, if the roots are very fine and fibrous, you will need to make a shallow cut with a sharp knife across the bottom of the root ball and about halfway up each side and then spread the roots to butterfly them slightly. This will encourage the roots to grow out of the circular pattern and into your soil.

Always water perennials in pots thoroughly before planting. If transplants are even slightly dry, they may be difficult to properly water once planted. If planted late in the season, transplants require very diligent watering for a good transition to pot or ground.

Handling Bare-Root Plants

Unpack bare-root perennials as soon as they arrive and plant right away. You may soak the roots for a few hours to help them regain moisture lost in shipping. Plant bare-root perennials while they are dormant; this will give the roots a chance to become established before new growth begins in spring. Bare-root perennials that are shipped too late—after their tops have begun to sprout—will need extra water and shade to ensure their survival in the garden. If possible, buy from a mail-order source whose shipping schedule coincides with your local planting dates, which is usually while deciduous trees are still bare.

Setting Plants in the Bed

Always set a plant at the same depth it was planted in its original container. The top of the root ball should be level with the surface of the soil. With bare-root plants it is more difficult to gauge the proper planting depth. If you look carefully, you can sometimes see a soil line on the plants, that is, a dirty or dark band of color. If this is not visible, plant so the **crown** (the point where the plant's top growth originates) sits just above soil level. Pat the soil around the plants firmly but do not pack it down. The idea is to eliminate air pockets and be sure the root ball is in firm contact with the soil.

Space transplants according to the directions on the label. Although spacing is never exact and will vary among selections of

Label your plants in the garden in order to know which selections are planted in a particular spot. This is especially helpful with plants that are new to you.

the same perennial, remember that plants placed too close together will compete for space. This will cause their stems to weaken as they stretch for light. Second to your experience, the plant label will provide you with the most accurate spacing information because it is selection specific. (If your plants are not labeled, shop where they are. Plants have traits specific to each selection that affect their successful placement.) Label plants in the garden, too, especially if you are planting new selections.

If you are planting a large bed, place plants in a staggered grid pattern rather than in even rows. This pattern ensures proper spacing and gives the bed a more organized look.

Care in the Garden

Perennials need water and food for growth and mulch to keep their roots moist. Given these, they will reward you with many years of color and texture.

Once you have prepared the soil and put your plants in the ground, taking care of your perennials involves water, fertilizer, and a bit of individual attention during the season. Your garden will be manageable and rewarding if you follow these steps from the start.

Watering

Perennials need more frequent watering when first planted. Later, established plants require less water, especially the more hardy species. Many methods of watering will work: a sprinkler, a soaker hose, or just a garden hose held over the plants. The key is to water thoroughly to encourage deep rooting. Shallow watering will keep roots close to the surface, making plants more susceptible to drought.

How much water is enough? Generally, an inch of water per application gets water deep enough in most soil types. You can measure an inch by placing several soup cans or inexpensive rain gauges in the range of your sprinkler (place pans under soaker hoses). When the containers have collected an inch of water, you will know how long it takes to deliver a proper application.

Do not apply an inch of water all at once if the bed is sloped or the soil drains poorly. Instead, apply until the water puddles or runs off, turn the sprinkler off for an hour or so to let the water soak in, and then reapply. Remember that sandy soils do not hold water well and will dry out more quickly than clay or rich soil.

You do not have to stand watch or come home early just to turn off your sprinkler. If you do not have an automatic irrigation system, you can install an inexpensive timer at the spigot. Models range from mechanical types that simply turn off the water after a set number of minutes (like a kitchen timer) to computerized types that program several days at a time (ideal when you are away on vacation).

Another way to make watering easier is to lay a soaker hose in the bed before setting out your transplants. Made of a porous material, a *soaker hose* allows water to seep out along its length. If the bed is longer than 20 feet, choose a hose less than ⅝ inch in diameter to ensure better pressure and thus a better flow of water along the length of the bed. Use snap-type couplers to make quick work of hooking and unhooking your garden hose to the soaker.

Getting water to your plants is made convenient by a variety of equipment.

Mulching

Mulch covers the ground like a blanket, helping deter the growth of weeds and keeping the soil moist. Organic mulches, such as bark, compost, and shredded leaves, build the richness of your soil as they decompose. Choose your mulch based on the terrain of your garden. Pine straw clings to gentle slopes better than other mulches because the needles knit together.

Apply the mulch 2 to 4 inches thick. The easiest way to mulch with pine straw is to apply the mulch before planting. After the soil is worked and raked smooth for planting, spread the mulch over the area. As you set out transplants, push a bit of the pine straw aside to clear a spot for each plant; this is easier than trying to knit the long needles together around and between plants after they are in the ground. If you use bark, compost, or other material that is easily spread, set transplants first and spread the mulch by hand or shovel between the plants. When transplants are small, you can cover each with a plastic cup and work quickly without fear of burying a plant. Simply lift the cups when the bed is mulched.

Mulch also helps protect plants from cold in winter. Half-hardy perennials, such as azure sage, may extend their range a bit farther north when covered with a layer of mulch.

Fertilizing

One look at the fertilizer shelf at the local garden center just might make you want to turn and run. With so many brands and formulas to choose from, you may feel a degree in chemistry would come in handy. However, if you arm yourself with a knowledge of what your plants need, you can feed your garden with minimal fuss.

The purpose of fertilization is to meet a plant's nutritional needs; these vary with both the age of the plant and the species. For example, a young plant generally needs nitrogen early in its life to support rapid growth. Later, as the plant reaches its full size, nitrogen becomes less important, and you can encourage blooms with a fertilizer high in phosphorus and potassium but lower in nitrogen. Some of today's hybrid perennials, such as improved daylilies, depend upon good fertilization to reach their full potential.

The easiest and most sensible approach to fertilization is to add adequate nutrients to the soil before you plant. In most cases, a good quality, slow-release fertilizer will suffice. If you have done a soil test, you are aware of any deficiencies or excesses that need correcting. Test results give specific recommendations to solve the problem.

To enrich your soil, you should always add compost or other organic matter that is rich in the many nutrients a plant needs.

Pine straw is one of the best mulching materials and is easily obtained by simply raking the fallen needles in late summer.

Then work a slow-release fertilizer into the soil before planting to ensure a constant supply of essential elements. If you use a chemical fertilizer, be sure to purchase one that contains at least half of its nitrogen in a timed-release form.

Organic gardeners may achieve similar results with organic fertilizers, such as blood meal or organic flower food, which depend upon soil bacteria to release their nitrogen as they decompose. These fertilizers yield good results and may increase microbial activity. Generally, organic fertilizers contain less nitrogen than their chemical counterparts. Blood meal is one of the highest in nitrogen, as it contains between 10 and 12 percent. Cottonseed meal contains about 6 percent nitrogen while composted chicken manure contains only 4 percent. If you compare cost per pound and quantity of nitrogen, organic fertilizers tend to be more expensive than their chemical counterparts.

To give young plants a boost, water them with a diluted fertilizer solution the first week or two after planting. This liquid food will be absorbed immediately. You may use an all-purpose formula on transplants.

The Fertilizer Label

By law, all fertilizers must carry a label stating the percentage of nutrients they contain. The three numbers always represent the percentage of nitrogen (N), phosphorus (P), and potassium (K). If the package says 10-5-8, it contains 10 percent nitrogen, 5 percent phosphorus, and 8 percent potassium. These are the nutrients most required by a plant, so the combination of nitrogen, phosphorus, and potassium makes up what is called a *complete fertilizer.*

Nitrogen stimulates new growth, especially foliage, which is why you need a good supply early in the growth cycle. Because it is very soluble and mobile in the soil, you should buy a product that contains a slow-release form. Otherwise, the nitrogen may be washed away before being absorbed.

Phosphorus encourages flowering and is essential for overall plant health; bloom-boosting fertilizers contain a high percentage of phosphorus. However, too much phosphorus in the soil blocks a plant's ability to absorb other nutrients. Unless you are gardening in containers or your soil test indicates a deficiency, use a fertilizer low in phosphorus. Many suburban soils may be high in phosphorus if the homes were built on land that was once agricultural. Liquid

Perennials in containers are completely dependent on you for fertilizer and water, as the soil in the pot is not as rich as that in the garden.

bloom-boosting products generally do not contribute to the buildup because they are diluted and are often sprayed directly on the foliage.

Potassium, also called potash on fertilizer labels, is essential to plant metabolism. It is crucial to a plant's cell wall structure as well as its ability to manufacture food. However, do not use potassium in excess as it may burn your plants.

Grooming Perennials

Tall perennials may need the support of a stake or grow-through wire mesh to keep them from falling over. The best time to set the support is when the plant is small so you do not risk breaking roots or stems by driving in a stake.

Certain plants will bloom longer if you remove the spent flowers before they can form seed. Those that respond well to **deadheading,** as this is called, include asters, mums, salvia, coreopsis, butterfly weed, and reblooming daylilies. Some perennials, such as blue star, peonies, astilbes, and most iris, only bloom once a year whether deadheaded or not.

A few perennials also need cutting back during the season to help them keep a neat form. For example, lamb's-ear will stretch and lose its matlike habit when the blooms appear; gardeners who object to this may snip the blooms off. Chrysanthemums are another example. They may grow too tall and leggy when left alone, but if trimmed back once or twice in spring and early summer, the plants will be fuller and neater and will produce more blooms.

If you snip the blooms off lamb's-ear when they appear, the plant will retain its matlike character.

Coreopsis will continue to produce buds and will bloom much longer if you trim off the spent blossoms before they produce seed.

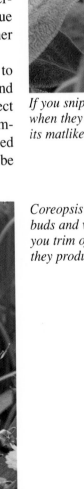

Propagating Perennials

Starting new plants is inherent to growing perennials, as many plants require digging and dividing to rejuvenate the planting. This makes perennials great for sharing with other gardeners. You may also start new plants from seed, a common way to add something new to your collection; however, these plants may not bloom until the second or third year.

Dividing

Because they live a long time and often form clumps or spread, it is easy to start new plants from existing perennials. This makes it economical to expand a planting or to give plants away. In fact, most perennials will bloom best if they are divided every three or four years, encouraging vigorous new shoots.

Perennials generally grow larger by sending out new shoots that arise from the base of the original. Hostas, arum, daylilies, daisies, mums, blue phlox, and many others grow this way, eventually forming a clump of multiple shoots or plantlets. To divide, simply dig the clump to separate the pieces. If the crown is dense and the roots are

Once you have a few perennials you will probably want more. Here is how to go about producing them.

To divide clumps of perennials with dense roots, such as hosta, you may need the help of a knife or a hatchet.

Shasta daisies spread by forming clumps that are easily lifted from the ground with a fork.

thick and tangled, the plants are not easy to separate. You will need a knife or a hatchet to cut through the tangled mass. As long as the plantlets you have divided still have their healthy shoots and roots intact, this will do them no harm.

After dividing, replant the smaller divisions or place them in pots to give away. Use this opportunity to rejuvenate the bed by adding organic matter to the soil.

Layering

Some perennials have stems that root where their *nodes,* or joints, touch the ground. Moss verbena and Bath's Pink dianthus are two examples. Often these plants root on their own as the stems creep, but if you want to encourage this, simply put a small rock over a node to ensure that it is in firm contact with the soil. Later, dig the newly rooted stem, cutting it away from the parent stem.

Starting from Seed

One of the advantages to growing your own perennial transplants is that you can grow selections that are otherwise not locally available. Sometimes this is the only way to obtain the plants you want. However, most perennials have very specific requirements for seed germination, so pick up a good book on seed propagation before you begin. Seed packets should also include any characteristics of the plant that will help you grow plants from seed.

A potting bench helps organize the items needed for propagating plants.

A Step-by-Step Method

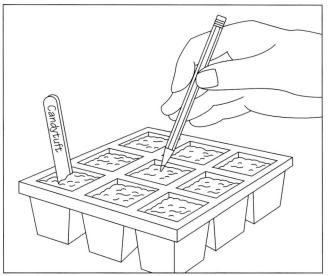

Sow seeds directly in a sterile container filled with a soil mix specially formulated for starting seeds. Be sure to water the flat before sowing. For fine seeds, use tweezers or the moistened tip of a pencil to place seeds in the containers; do not bury the seeds, but press them firmly into the mix.

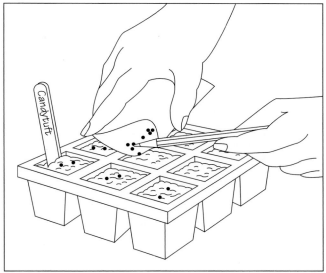

Sow two seeds in each cell for insurance. Be sure to label each pack with the name of the perennial and the planting date. Flat wooden sticks and a fine-tip permanent marker work well.

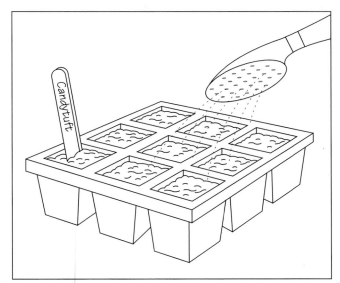

Keep the flat watered with the fine spray of a watering can. To conserve moisture, place the flat in a clear plastic bag, but remove it when the seedlings appear. Do not use a bag if you place the flat on a warm surface, such as a water heater.

In all likelihood, more than one seed will germinate. When this occurs, snip off the smaller seedling at the soil level with nail scissors.

Plant Hardiness Zone Map

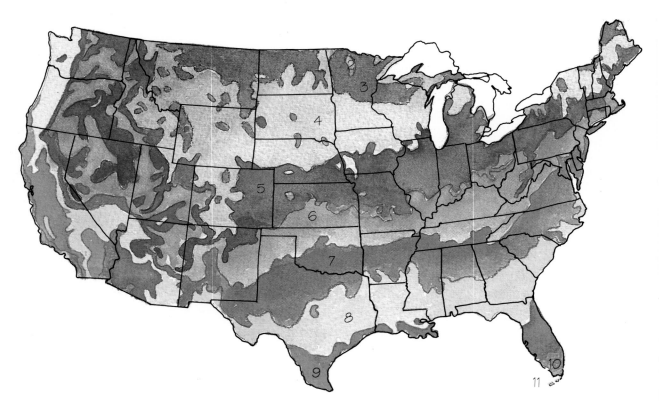

The United States Department of Agriculture has charted low temperatures throughout the country to determine the ranges of average low readings. The map above is based loosely on the USDA Plant Hardiness Zone Map, which was drawn from these findings. It does not take into account heat, soil, or moisture extremes and is intended as a guide, not a guarantee.

The southern regions of the United States that are mentioned in this book refer to the following:

Upper South: Zone 6

Middle South: upper region of Zone 7 (0 to 5 degrees minimum)

Lower South: lower region of Zone 7 and upper region of Zone 8 (5 to 15 degrees minimum)

Coastal South: lower region of Zone 8 and upper region of Zone 9 (15 to 25 degrees minimum)

Tropical South: lower region of Zone 9 and all of Zone 10 (25 to 40 degrees minimum)

Zone 2	-50	to	-40°F
Zone 3	-40	to	-30°F
Zone 4	-30	to	-20°F
Zone 5	-20	to	-10°F
Zone 6	-10	to	0°F
Zone 7	0	to	10°F
Zone 8	10	to	20°F
Zone 9	20	to	30°F
Zone 10	30	to	40°F
Zone 11		above	40°F

Plant Profiles

The perennials described in the following pages were selected by the garden editors at *Southern Living* on the basis of their beauty, adaptability, and value in the garden. They represent a wide spectrum of perennials, from those that thrive anywhere—in full sun and sandy soil—to those that need rich soil and regular attention. Many are tried-and-true favorites that have worked for gardeners for years.

Arranged alphabetically by common name, these profiles give you a description of each plant, information about planting and propagating, and suggested ways that you can incorporate its color, height, and form into your garden. The profile also suggests companion plants that mix well with each perennial.

Critical to your success is knowing the soil and cultural conditions a plant needs; this information is contained in the profiles, along with tips for keeping the plant looking its best and troubleshooting solutions to help you fight any pests or diseases.

When a genus contains more than one related species, such as coreopsis, the group is combined in a single entry. The profile points out the differences in appearance and growing needs of the most popular species and hybrids.

For a quick overview of the plant, refer to the *At a Glance* box that accompanies every profile. This will give you the major features of the perennial, such as its soil and light requirements. The box also includes the plant's botanical name to help you avoid confusion when buying perennials.

Try experimenting with new perennials in your garden each year. Feel free to plant those that you have never grown before or that are only marginally suited to your climate.

You will find a natural variation among plants growing under different conditions. For example, flower colors are brighter in cool, crisp weather; plants often stretch taller in shade than they would grow in sun; and most are shorter in hot, dry climates. All this is a normal part of plant response, so keep it in mind when local information is different from what you see or read here.

Coneflowers and salvia

Arum

After arum's leaves die back in late spring, red berries appear on the old flower stalks.

AT A GLANCE

❖

ARUM
Arum italicum

Features: striking winter foliage color and texture

Colors: mottled dark green leaves with white flowers and red berries

Height: 12 to 20 inches

Light: partial to deep shade

Soil: moist, rich

Water: medium

Pests: none specific

Native: no

Range: Zones 6 to 9

Remarks: reseeds, making it a great plant for sharing

Arum looks like a small tropical plant, but it is at its peak during the coldest time of year. Few perennials are more intriguing in both looks and behavior. Not only does arum's foliage pop through the soil in fall, a time when most things are about to die back, but the unusual leaves also endure freeze after freeze until warm weather arrives.

In late fall, green-and-white arrow-shaped leaves emerge, each almost a foot long and as rippled and exotic as crocodile skin. The foliage is hardy in all regions of the South. Even if very cold weather appears to have damaged the plant, the leaves will sprout anew. But most gardeners can count on its interesting presence all winter long.

In spring, pale green callalike flowers appear, reminiscent of jack-in-the-pulpit. In late spring, the leaves will die back as the plant goes dormant. Then, in early summer, a short stalk of glossy red berries may appear on two- to three-year-old plants that receive bright light.

In the Landscape

Use arum under trees and in other shady spots. It is quite tolerant of deep shade and makes a nice winter blanket in the shade. Use arum to beautify the winter garden by planting it in groups on the north side of your house for a focal point along a walkway or a patio. It is also a hard-working winter ground cover that contrasts handsomely with other evergreens or plants with winter interest, such as Lenten rose or evergreen ferns. If planted in a moist, shady location, arum will slowly spread to be a handsome ground cover.

Combine arum with hostas for year-round ground cover. The hostas will cover the ground from spring into summer while the arum is dormant. Caladiums are another good summer companion, but be careful not to damage arum's roots when planting caladium tubers.

Different Selections

Although few named selections are commonly found, one called Pictum has particularly handsome silver markings on the foliage and is a bit more variegated than the white-veined species.

The exotic-looking leaves of arum are unexpected from a cold-hardy winter perennial.

Planting and Care

Plant arum in partial shade in moist, rich soil. If you let the seeds ripen and fall to the ground, they will be the source of new seedlings to share. You may also divide the plant in fall by separating the clumps of leaves as they break through the ground. Dig carefully and deeply, as the fleshy foliage is easily broken away from the roots and then the bulbous root becomes nearly impossible to find.

Aster

Daisylike blooms with yellow centers characterize all asters. This selection is Harrington's Pink.

Because of their hardy nature and royal autumn show, asters are on the "must have" list of many veteran gardeners, and rightly so. Just when summer has taken its toll on much of the garden, asters begin to bloom—quietly at first, opening only a few blossoms, and then showering the garden with daisylike flowers in white, blue, purple, lavender, pink, and even yellow. As the nights get cooler in September and October, the colors of the flowers intensify.

In the Landscape

Asters vary from 6 inches to 7 feet tall, allowing for many uses in the garden. Taller asters are perfect for late summer and fall color at the back of a flower border, while dwarf selections can edge a border or even comprise a mass planting. Asters are also popular used singly sprinkled through a rock garden. Often purchased in full bloom, asters create instant color in containers or window boxes and can be transplanted to the garden after the blooms fade.

Asters can certainly stand by themselves, but their beauty is perhaps most fully realized when they are combined with other fall-blooming perennials. Grow them alongside goldenrod, Formosa lily, and blue or purple salvias. Other useful late-blooming companions include ornamental grasses, mums, boltonia, and Mexican mint marigold. Many selections also make excellent cut flowers.

Tatarian aster grows to 7 feet and works well at the back of a fall flower border.

Species and Selections

Open any catalog and you will see at least a half-dozen different improved selections. New aster cultivars are introduced every year, so shop around for different colors, heights, and foliage. Often they are selections of one of the following major types.

New England aster *(Aster novae-angliae)* is also native to the South, despite its name. Selections range from 3 to 5 feet in height. While most bloom in some shade of purple, New England asters may also be red or pink. Most bloom in September and October, but Harrington's Pink and Alma Potschke (deep rose) begin blooming in midsummer with flowers that are 2 inches across. Autumn Snow is a late-blooming white, a rare color among this group of asters.

New York aster *(Aster novi-belgii)*, also called Michaelmas daisy, is the parent plant of many hybrid asters. This species is also a Southern native and typically grows 3 to 4 feet tall with blue-violet blooms. Hybrids feature single, semidouble, or double flowers of white, lavender, pink, blue, rose, purple, or red. Heights range from the 10 or 12 inches of the selection Professor Anton Kippenburg to the 48 inches of Coombe Violet. Most selections bloom in September and October, but some bloom earlier. As cut flowers they are superior to New England asters, which close soon after cutting.

Skydrop aster *(Aster patens)*, another native, deserves much wider use. It grows 2 to 3 feet tall and bears bright violet-blue flowers on delicate, upright stems. Like all true asters, its blossoms sport yellow centers. It is very late blooming and quite tolerant of dry fall weather.

Aromatic aster *(Aster oblongifolius)* grows to a bushy mound about 2 feet high. Lavender flowers appear atop leaves that are pleasantly fragrant when crushed. This native plant is durable, drought tolerant, and trouble free, and it is among the latest asters to bloom, usually in November.

Tatarian aster *(Aster tataricus)* adds impact to the garden with leaves that may be 2 feet long and spikes of pale blue-purple flowers that top 7-foot stems. Although it is not a native plant, it is quite dependable and thrives in sandy or heavy soils. Blooming quite late, often into November, it is striking when massed at the back of the border; it may be paired with tall ornamental grasses for a lovely natural look. Tatarian aster needs a sturdy stake to keep it from falling over. Jindai is a lower growing selection that matures at only 4 feet tall and is less likely to need staking than other asters.

There are many selections of the dependable New England asters, ranging from 3 to 5 feet.

Weighted by rain, the lanky stems of tatarian aster rest on sedum Autumn Joy.

Golden aster (Aster linosyris) is a bright, cheery aster that grows 18 to 20 inches tall and bears yellow blooms in late summer and early fall.

Frikart's aster (Aster x frikartii) is a mildew-resistant, long-blooming plant that bears its lavender flowers much earlier than other asters, typically in early to midsummer, and continues to bloom for weeks if you remove the dead flowers. In the lower and coastal South it generally behaves as an annual.

Planting and Care

Asters prefer full sun but will tolerate light shade. Some grow well in dry soil, but most like consistent moisture. Good drainage is essential. These perennials do well throughout the South except near the coast, where summer heat and humidity may cause the plants to rot. The height of tall asters can be a problem in small gardens. To keep these plants a manageable size, cut them back by 6 inches in the spring and in midsummer. You will have shorter, stockier plants that bloom in the fall and should not need to be staked.

Divide plants every two to three years to keep them vigorous. Divide in early spring or fall, lifting each clump and separating the youngest asters to replant; discard the old center.

Troubleshooting

Powdery mildew plagues the foliage of many asters in spring and fall. See page 125 for more about powdery mildew.

Golden aster departs from the usual pink and lavender to sport blooms of rich yellow in late summer and early autumn.

Dwarf asters are perfect for a rock garden, an edging, or the front of a border.

Astilbe

Gardeners who grow astilbe treasure the ephemeral beauty and stunning color it brings to the summer shade garden. And despite rumors that it is finicky, astilbe performs well in the South.

Several species of astilbe, which is native to China and Japan, thrive in shade in the South. Their feathery pink, peach, red, or white plumes soften and decorate the landscape like icing on a cake. In the southern limit of astilbe's range, the feathery flower spikes appear in midspring, while farther north they usually wait until summer. Flowers appear from mid-May through August, but astilbe's fernlike foliage—ranging from deep green to copper—exudes a quiet elegance for months on end.

In the Landscape

Plants range from 1 to 4 feet in height, with shorter selections for the front of the garden and taller plants for the back of the border, with no staking needed. Plant a mass of astilbe in a shady bed to create a summer focal point, or plant three in the corner of a shady border for a colorful accent. Since astilbe enjoys moist soil, it is great for grouping near birdbaths, ponds, and other water features.

Try astilbes in large sweeps for dramatic effect or combine them in a perennial border with other plants that need similar growing conditions. Combine them with hostas, goldenray, Japanese anemones, stokesia, and dead nettle, all of which bring color and texture to shade.

Astilbe works well with hostas in a perennial border, as both plants prefer shade and moist, well-drained soil.

Deep pink is one of the more popular shades of astilbe.

AT A GLANCE

❖

ASTILBE
Astilbe species and hybrids

Features: colorful summer plumes, fine-textured foliage for shade

Colors: pink, red, peach, white, lavender

Height: 1 to 4 feet

Light: filtered morning sun or afternoon shade

Soil: moist, well drained

Water: high

Pests: none specific

Native: no

Range: Zones 4 to 8

Remarks: bears excellent flowers for cutting and nice foliage when not in bloom

The soft white blooms of this astilbe fall gracefully into a path as they reach for light.

Plant astilbes where they may be easily observed because their flowers have such richness and intricacy of detail that they merit close observation. They make excellent cut flowers if the blooms are harvested just after they open. Left on the plant, the flower spikes remain ornamental, even after blooming has ceased. And after the foliage and flowers die down, the seed heads that appear are also attractive, making astilbe a plant of many seasons.

Species and Selections

Astilbe (*Astilbe* x *arendsii*) is the most common group of hybrids. These plants bloom for at least three weeks and grow 1 to 4 feet tall, depending on the selection. Selections include Fanal, which blooms in deep red, Deutschland, which blooms in white, and Rheinland, which bears pink blooms; these selections mature at 2 feet tall. Red Sentinel is a 3-foot plant that blooms in bright red; Purple Blaze is a 4-foot plant with purple blooms.

Peach Blossom (*Astilbe* x *rosea* Peach Blossom) is a vigorous, 3- to 4-foot-tall hybrid that features showy salmon pink flowers in midspring.

Chinese astilbe (*Astilbe chinensis*) is a late-blooming species that will make a handsome ground cover as it spreads by underground stems. Pumila is a selection that grows 12 to 18 inches tall; it has lavender-pink flower spikes that are dusted with a bluish-silver hue.

Fall astilbe (*Astilbe taquetii*) is a rather tall species (up to 4 feet) that bears purple flowers in mid- to late summer. These blooms are especially nice for cutting. Fall astilbe is better adapted to the warm weather of the lower and coastal South than other species.

Planting and Care

Astilbes flourish throughout the South, except in the hottest parts. If you live in the lower and coastal South, you can grow astilbes, although the plants will not be as vigorous as they are in areas where they can get a longer winter rest. In fact, they may only live a year or two unless planted in a cool spot with plenty of moisture.

These perennials prefer deep, rich soil. Steady moisture is a must, particularly in summer. For that reason, astilbes should be planted in areas that can be watered in times of drought. Do not allow soil to dry out. They are not bog plants, however. They only like water when they are actively growing. If the soil is wet in winter, astilbes will rot.

Plant astilbes in either strong, filtered light or morning sun and afternoon shade. The farther south you live, the more shade astilbes require, though it should never be dense. Astilbes are heavy feeders and respond well to spring applications of slow-release flower food.

Every three years or so, dig up the plants, divide them, and replant. Not only does this give you more plants, but it keeps them vigorous and blooming freely. Astilbe is a long-lived perennial when provided good conditions.

Long-lived and dependable, astilbe is a staple of flower borders.

The tall flower spikes of Fanal draw attention to any shady location. The flowers remain attractive even after they fade.

Begonia

Hardy begonia's unusual blooms bring a soft shade of pink to the garden in late summer and fall.

One of the most surprising perennials for the Southern garden in late summer and fall is hardy begonia. Most gardeners do not expect a begonia to be perennial because the most common ones are annual, but this antique plant can be counted on to come back faithfully and reseed year after year in Zones 7 and 8, the warmer part of its range.

With its tropical-looking leaves and tubular flamingo-colored blooms, hardy begonia fills in shaded corners of the garden and attracts pleasant inquiries from passersby not familiar with its old-fashioned charm.

In the Landscape

Shade is a must for hardy begonia, which grows from 12 to 24 inches tall and has a loose, mounding form built on arching, fleshy stems. Its 3- to 6-inch, light green leaves have red undersides, which makes them interesting when planted at the edge of a wall or other place where the underside of the plant can be seen. Their texture is coarse and contrasts well with the finer leaves of other shade-loving plants, such as astilbes or ferns.

Hardy begonia also blends well in a naturalistic planting with Lenten rose and hosta. You may even use it as a seasonal ground cover under trees, interspersed with Italian arum or daffodils to take its place in winter when the foliage has died down. It also pairs well with tropical plants such as impatiens and ginger lily. Hardy begonia is an attractive plant for the front of the border; its heart-shaped leaves will gently arch over walkway edges. Because it will spread by reseeding, hardy begonia is a good choice for untended areas where the plants are able to spread as they may.

AT A GLANCE
❖
HARDY BEGONIA
Begonia grandis

Features: colorful, heart-shaped leaves; late summer flowers

Colors: pink

Height: 12 to 24 inches

Light: partial shade

Soil: rich, light, well drained

Water: medium

Pests: none specific

Native: no

Range: Zones 6 to 8

Remarks: nice texture for shade, even when not in bloom

Planting and Care

Hardy begonia needs rich soil with good drainage and must have protection from the hot midday and afternoon sun. Hardy begonias will flourish for years, even decades, if planted in the right location. Hardy begonias thrive in Zones 7 and 8 where winter is not too cold but is cool enough to provide the necessary period of dormancy. In Zone 6, you may plant them in a protected spot or mulch with pine straw or bark to protect tubers from the cold. Farther north, dig the plants in the fall and replant in the late spring, after the threat of frost is past.

You may dig plants when they first come up in spring to give away or to transplant to other parts of the garden. However, hardy begonia does not require dividing to keep it vigorous as many other perennials do. It reproduces by seed and tiny bulbs that form on the leaves; seedlings often need more than one year to bloom.

Hardy begonia fills shady corners with its lush foliage and colorful blooms.

Bleeding Heart

White bleeding heart brings light to a dark woodland floor.

Gardeners prize bleeding heart for its delicate blooms that dangle like bracelet charms in spring. The first part of its name is derived from the inner petals that "drip" from the tip of the heart-shaped outer petals and resemble a drop of blood (albeit white). The arching flower stems held above the foliage provide a charming companion to other shade-loving spring flowers, such as blue forget-me-nots. Two of the most popular species of bleeding heart are common bleeding heart, whose foliage dies down soon after the plant blooms, and fringed bleeding heart, a native whose foliage remains all summer.

In the Landscape

Because it is sure to be a conversation piece, place bleeding heart in a spot where it will be seen. Plant common bleeding heart in combination with compatible plants, such as ferns and hostas, that will fill the void when it disappears. Its wildflower-like qualities make it an excellent choice for wooded gardens in combination with daffodils, ferns, woodland phlox, hostas, and other shade-loving perennials.

Common bleeding heart forms a clump of loose, open, parsleylike foliage that is often floppy; for that reason, it looks best when planted in groups of three or more for a fuller look. However, the foliage of fringed bleeding heart is fuller and the stems are stiffer so the plant does not flop. In fact, fringed bleeding heart keeps its foliage until fall if you do not let it dry out in summer.

Species and Selections

Common bleeding heart was introduced from Japan more than 100 years ago and has become a garden classic. This long-lived perennial is well adapted to growing conditions throughout the South except the arid regions of Texas and south Florida. In early spring the plants send up soft, bright green leaves. Later the flowering begins, with rose or white blossoms gradually unfolding from bottom to top

---

AT A GLANCE
❖
COMMON BLEEDING HEART
Dicentra spectabilis

Features: arching sprays of heart-shaped blooms

Colors: pink, white

Height: 1 to 2 feet

Light: shade

Soil: moist, rich, acid

Water: high

Pests: none specific

Native: no

Range: Zones 2 to 8

Remarks: goes dormant and disappears in summer

along long arching racemes. After the flowers fall, the foliage turns yellow and gradually disappears; by midsummer, the plant is completely gone until the next year, which is why it is best to pair it with longer lasting plants.

A surprising selection of common bleeding heart is the pure white Pantaloons, which grows larger and blooms more than another popular white selection, Alba.

Fringed bleeding heart is native to the South and has more elongated, lighter pink blossoms than common bleeding heart. Its blooms are also more crowded on the flowering stem, tending to lose the attractive effect of common bleeding heart's blooms. Although most gardeners prefer the rounded flowers and more graceful habit of common bleeding heart, fringed bleeding heart does have two superior qualities: it continues to bloom sporadically on branched flower stems throughout the summer, and the foliage does not die back until autumn unless the soil dries out. This makes it an excellent summer ground cover for shady areas.

Hybrid selections of fringed bleeding heart include Luxuriant, a 15-inch-tall plant named for its lush, green, long-lasting foliage; it has deep reddish-pink blooms that appear sporadically through summer. Boothman's Variety has light pink flowers. Snowdrift has white blossoms and gray-green foliage.

Planting and Care

Bleeding heart needs moist, acid soil that is rich in organic matter. Before planting, work plenty of sphagnum peat moss, compost, or leaf mold into the bed. Set plants so that the crown is slightly above ground level and not covered with soil. If you purchase plants through the mail and they arrive with bare roots, you must set them out immediately.

Partial shade is also a requirement; if not shaded, the foliage will burn. Water bleeding heart frequently during dry weather, as even the long-lasting foliage of fringed bleeding heart will die if the soil dries out.

Bleeding heart will continue to bloom for many years without being divided, but if you want to start new plants or give them away, you may take root cuttings in summer or fall. You may also sow seeds of fringed bleeding heart in late summer; the seeds will sit in the bed through winter and germinate in early spring after exposure to cold.

Fringed bleeding heart has finely cut, long-lasting foliage and blooms that are borne on branched flower stems.

AT A GLANCE
FRINGED BLEEDING HEART
Dicentra eximia

Features: sprays of heart-shaped blooms
Colors: pink, white
Height: 1 to 2 feet
Light: shade
Soil: moist, rich, acid
Water: high
Pests: none specific
Native: yes
Range: Zones 2 to 8
Remarks: continues blooming until fall

Bluebell

Flower buds of bluebells emerge as a lavender pink.

A native of the Eastern woodlands, Virginia bluebells bring a rare bundle of blue to the shade garden in early spring, about the time woodland phlox and violets bloom. Lifted on slender stalks above soft, green foliage, the flowers of Virginia bluebells form pastel clusters that bow their heads toward the earth. The buds emerge a lavender pink and then deepen to sky blue as the bell-shaped blossoms open. The result is a constantly changing color combination that adds charm to a perennial border or a woodland garden for several weeks in March or April. But however beautiful, bluebells are brief; in a few weeks their foliage dies back and all signs of the plant disappear until the next spring.

In the Landscape

Virginia bluebells grow from 18 inches to 2 feet in height and can be used in a number of ways. Because their foliage yellows and completely vanishes by late spring or early summer, you will want to mix them with other plants or use them in a location where the yellowing foliage does not matter.

You might plant Virginia bluebells in a natural setting, such as a large sweep along a creek bank, or as underplantings for azaleas, rhododendrons, or other evergreen shrubs. Many gardeners plant Virginia bluebells with other native perennials, such as columbine, to conceal the bluebells' foliage. For a striking combination, try planting yellow daffodils or early-blooming pastel tulips with bluebells. The same bed may also hold summer ferns and hostas, whose foliage will emerge in late spring to fill the void left by the bluebells. Or bunch a few plants together in a place where their delicate flowers can be appreciated at close range and mix them with summer annuals, such as impatiens. Wherever you plant bluebells, you may wish to place a small marker lest you forget they are there while the plants are dormant.

Different Selections

This plant is not easy to find in garden centers because it is available for such a short time. The best time to find it is in early spring when the plants are in bloom. Chances are, you will have to order plants from a mail-order source. Most of what is offered are seedlings of the species. However, breeders have developed two cultivars, Alba, a white selection, and Rubra, a pink.

Planting and Care

Virginia bluebells are native to moist woodland soils, often near streams, and will do best where there is shade, rich soil, and plenty of moisture in the spring. Given these conditions, they are among the most reliable perennials for home gardens in all but the coastal South. They can tolerate full sun because the sun is not strong while their foliage is present.

If you see Virginia bluebells blooming in the forest, do not dig them up to bring home. Because their tubers are deep rooted and brittle, your chances for success are very slight. Start with nursery-grown transplants that you set out in spring or plant dormant tubers in fall. Before planting, amend the soil by working in plenty of compost, sphagnum peat moss, or rotted manure. Plant so that the tops of the large tubers are about 4 inches below ground, and space both tubers and plants about 12 inches apart.

Once established, Virginia bluebells need very little care. Make sure they get plenty of water, and each spring before the leaves emerge, apply compost as mulch or top dressing to supply nutrients and to replenish organic matter in the soil. After the flowers fade, the foliage quickly yellows; you must leave the leaves intact to nourish the underground tubers.

When paired with apricot-colored tulips, Virginia bluebells make a stunning show in the spring.

Blue Star

Blue star is named for its five-petaled, star-shaped blooms.

Native to the South and the Midwest, blue star includes several species of the genus *Amsonia,* known for its steel blue flowers in the spring and, in some cases, bright yellow leaves in the fall. The show begins in early spring, when stems carrying narrow, willowlike leaves sprout from a crown at the base of the plant. When fully grown, the plant stands 2 to 3 feet tall with a 3- to 4-foot spread. Clusters of steel blue, star-shaped flowers appear atop the foliage in mid- to late spring, lasting for two to four weeks.

In autumn, the foliage of blue star changes to yellow or orange-yellow. Curiously, the leaf color is usually more intense in the South than in the North. The blossoms also make fine cut flowers. Clusters of slender, milkweedlike pods appear in midsummer and may be used in flower arrangements. And the colorful foliage can be used in autumn arrangements, too.

In the Landscape

Few perennials can match blue star's versatility in the garden. It blooms equally well in sun and light shade, and it is resilient, coming back year after year without division or a lot of fuss. It is a choice plant in a border, as an informal hedge, or for naturalizing. Blue star is open enough to let you see other plants behind it. You can combine it with peonies, irises, columbines, lamb's-ears, and tulips in a sunny border. Or plant it in a woodland garden next to ferns, hostas, primroses, daffodils, and spring wildflowers.

Species and Selections

Several species of blue star are good garden flowers. All grow in Zones 3 to 9 except sandhills blue star, which is not hardy in cold climates.

Willow amsonia *(Amsonia tabernaemontana)* is named for its willowlike leaves that turn yellow in fall, just like the willow tree. It grows to about 3 feet tall. Dwarf blue star *(Amsonia tabernaemontana montana)* is a selection that grows only 15 to 18 inches tall and boasts full clusters of darker blue flowers than the species. Salicifolia is a selection with long, narrow leaves and silvery-blue flowers with white throats.

Arkansas blue star *(Amsonia hubrectii)* is a lovely plant that resembles dwarf blue star but grows slightly taller. It has thin, threadlike leaves that have beautiful yellow fall color and contrast nicely with shade-loving plants, such as hardy begonia.

AT A GLANCE
❖
BLUE STAR
Amsonia species

Features: airy, star-shaped flowers atop tall, willowy foliage

Colors: blue flowers, golden fall foliage

Height: 1½ to 3 feet

Light: full sun or light shade

Soil: moist, rich, well drained

Water: medium

Pests: none specific

Native: yes

Range: Zones 3 to 9

Remarks: excellent for naturalizing or for country or cottage gardens

Sandhills blue star, or feather amsonia *(Amsonia angustifolia)*, sports more narrow leaves than blue star and tolerates drier soil. It is also called downy amsonia for the hairy new leaves that give the plant a soft, silky look. Like willow amsonia, sandhills blue star also has bright yellow fall color. This is the least cold hardy of all blue stars, but it does endure the hot, humid climate of the coastal South, growing well in Zones 7 to 9.

Planting and Care

Plant blue star in full sun to partial shade in rich, moist soil. Plants in shade may need to be cut back to about half their height at least once after they bloom to keep them from growing too gangly. Once it is established, you can divide blue star in fall or spring to give away or start a new plant in another spot. However, the clumps will grow and bloom dependably for many years without being divided.

To start the plants from seed, you should sow in the fall to give them exposure to cold weather. Seeds do not germinate very dependably, so it is easier to start from transplants when possible.

Blue star blooms well in sun or shade. It sparkles amid ferns and Allegheny pachysandra in a woodland garden.

A native wildflower, blue star's fresh spring blooms also make long-lasting cut flowers.

Boltonia

Boltonia blossoms look like tiny daisies.

Boltonia is a native plant that proves summer flowers do not have to end with the sultry days of August. This mounding perennial is covered with hundreds of asterlike blooms in white, pale pink, or purple that are cool and fresh in the heat of summer. The plant's narrow leaves are nearly concealed by the flowers.

In the Landscape

In the wild, boltonia is a tall, lanky plant that many people consider too weedy to add to a garden. However, the improved selections are a bit shorter, generally 3 to 4 feet tall, and more tame. Use them on slopes, in meadow plantings, or with ornamental grasses for a natural effect. Because boltonia lightens and brightens the garden, it can draw attention to a dark corner or enhance an area that is used at night. Pair white boltonia with blue or lavender asters for a refreshing combination. Wild seedlings tend to look a bit weedy and should be reserved for wildflower gardens.

Different Selections

Snowbank is by far the most widely grown selection because it maintains a fairly compact form—3 to 4 feet in height—and delights gardeners with its mass of airy white blooms. Be prepared to support the plant with raffia or other tie to help withstand bad weather. Pink Beauty is a pale pink selection that is shorter than the wild species but may grow to 5 feet in height and will need staking. Its foliage has a handsome bluish cast.

Planting and Care

Although boltonia enjoys good garden soil amended with organic matter, it is quite tolerant of drought. In fact, it prefers dry conditions to wet ones, so make sure the soil is well drained. Plant in full or

AT A GLANCE

BOLTONIA
Boltonia asteroides

Features: asterlike flowers in late summer and fall

Colors: white, pale pink

Height: 3 to 7 feet

Light: full or morning sun

Soil: rich, well drained

Water: low to medium

Pests: none specific

Native: yes

Range: Zones 4 to 8

Remarks: also does well in dry soil

morning sun. Boltonia will tolerate afternoon shade but becomes a stronger, more compact plant in full sun. Plants grown in shade may require staking. In the lower South, boltonia needs protection from the late afternoon sun.

In late summer when the first flush of blooms turns brown, cut back half of the stems and they will bloom again in a few weeks. A clump of boltonia will multiply at the base, making propagation by division easy. Divide clumps every third or fourth fall to keep the plants vigorous. Hybrid selections, such as Snowbank, will not come true from seed; however, the native wild type can be started from seeds collected from the plants in autumn. Sow right away for best results.

Snowbank, a prized white selection, wins hearts to boltonia in late summer and early fall.

Butterfly Weed

Although named for the butterflies that are so fond of its nectar-rich flowers, butterfly weed also attracts bees.

Like other flowers that thrive on hot, windswept roadsides, butterfly weed is among the most durable plants in nature. It is also one of the showiest, blooming a hot red, orange, or yellow in late spring and summer throughout the South. Growing on bushy plants that are 1 to 3 feet tall, the flowers will last for up to six weeks. Gardeners have come to appreciate this plant's stamina and the butterflies it attracts, for these insects like to sip nectar from the colorful blossoms, giving butterfly weed its name. It is also a host plant for monarch and queen butterflies, who lay their eggs on the foliage so that the hatching caterpillars can feed on the leaves.

The blooms of butterfly weed are also valued for use as cut flowers, which easily last a week or more.

In the Landscape

Although it grows wild along roadsides and other hot, dry areas, butterfly weed loves the moist, rich soil of a flower bed, forming 2- to 3-foot clumps. Plant it in combination with yellow daylilies or deep blue veronicas for impact, or with perennial butterfly bush *(Buddleia species)* or annual lantana, which are other plants that teem with butterflies. Butterfly weed has deep green, leathery foliage and stiff, upright stems that give it a shrublike appearance. Use it singly as an accent in a bed of low-growing, finely textured ground cover.

Flower arrangers often include butterfly weed in a bed for cutting. Cut the blooms early in the morning or at night, and set the stems in water almost up to the flowers. Snipping flowers from the plant also increases the number of blooms.

Species and Selections

Gay Butterflies is the most popular selection of butterfly weed, made up of a mix of yellow, orange, and red flowers. Plants grow 2 to 2½ feet tall.

Swamp milkweed *(Asclepias incarnata)* is a close relative of butterfly weed and is native to moist soils from Canada to Florida and westward to Utah. Unlike butterfly weed, swamp milkweed will tolerate boggy, poorly drained soil; however, it will also grow in typical garden conditions without extra water. Its flowers are a soft white and are borne atop 3- to 5-foot-tall stems that may need staking during heavy rain. It does not have a long taproot and thus is easier to transplant than butterfly weed. The flowers of swamp milkweed are also prized for cutting. Ice Ballet is a selection that grows to about 4 feet tall.

Planting and Care

Butterfly weed will grow in full sun and poor soil, including dry, sandy sites. However, it will form larger clumps in better soil. Good drainage is also a must.

Butterfly weed is among the last perennials to peek through the soil in spring, so do not give up. It also takes two to three years to reach full size; first-year plants will be small. Container-grown plants are easiest to transplant if they are young. In the garden, the plant will develop a taproot, making transplanting difficult after a year or two. Digging plants from the roadside is not a good idea because their taproots are mired in gravel and compacted soil. Instead, collect a few seeds from the mature pods in late summer.

Because this plant is a host for butterflies, you will find caterpillars feeding on the foliage of butterfly weed. Leave them to feed if you want to enjoy the adult butterflies; the plant will not be affected.

Starting from Seed

To gather seeds, pick an entire pod when it first begins to split. Strip the silky fibers from the seeds, and you are ready to plant. For best results, sow seeds immediately after you collect them; dried seeds do not germinate well. Seedlings will quickly develop a long taproot, so it is best to plant them directly in a garden bed. If you would rather plant the seeds in a container, transplant them into the garden or their own containers as soon as the first true leaves appear. (Turn to page 30 to read more about seed sowing.) These plants should bloom in their second season.

When seedpods turn brown and split open, rows of seeds are set free. The wind catches their silken parachutes and carries them far from the mother plant.

Butterfly weed blooms in late spring and summer throughout the South.

53

Candytuft

Spring transforms the glossy, evergreen mounds of candytuft foliage into frothy masses of pure white blossoms.

AT A GLANCE
CANDYTUFT
Iberis sempervirens

Features: evergreen, low-growing plant with spring blooms

Colors: white

Height: 4 to 12 inches

Light: full sun to partial shade

Soil: well drained

Water: low

Pests: none specific

Native: no

Range: Zones 3 to 9

Remarks: excellent plant for edgings or rock gardens

Candytuft is a hardy evergreen perennial that is tolerant of cold, heat, and drought, bearing perfectly formed white spring blooms that bring to mind after-dinner mints. The blossoms, which open in early spring, last several weeks, and some selections will bloom again in the fall. Candytuft's dark green, glossy foliage lends color, texture and cascading form year-round when it is used as a ground cover.

In the Landscape

Because of its low, spreading habit (6 to 8 inches), candytuft is best used in edgings, flower borders, or rock gardens, or as a ground cover. For dramatic contrast in both color and form, plant evergreen candytuft as a foreground for vertical, strongly colored flowers, such as deep blue iris or rich red tulips. It also makes a handsome companion for annuals and bulbs that bloom at the same time, such as pansies and tulips. White-blooming selections may be used to tie together a mix of varied spring colors. As a ground cover, it can be used along the edge of a bed of taller shrubs, such as azaleas, for a double display of color.

The glossy evergreen foliage of candytuft is a nice ground cover even after the blooms have faded. You can interplant late-flowering bulbs, such as spider lily or autumn crocus, in clumps among the evergreen leaves.

Different Selections

Several named selections of evergreen candytuft are available in a variety of sizes. Reaching a height of about 7 inches are Purity, Christmas Snow (which blooms again in autumn), and Snowflake (bearing large flowers). Two smaller selections are Pygmea (4 inches tall) and Little Gem (5 inches). Plants generally spread at least two to three times their height.

Planting and Care

Candytuft needs a sunny spot and well-drained soil. It will also tolerate light shade, but you should never plant it in poorly drained soil or the plant will rot in winter. In fact, rot is the worst enemy of candytuft, as diseases and insects are seldom problems. If your soil is very heavy, improve drainage by working in a generous amount of organic matter, such as compost or manure.

To keep your plants growing vigorously and looking compact, trim them back several inches once blooming has stopped.

Fall is the time to divide candytuft, should you want to start new plantings. Since the stems naturally spread and root easily in moist soil, simply sever the stem, lift out a piece, and plant. You can start candytuft from seed, but setting out purchased transplants or divisions is easier.

Candytuft is a good companion to thrift, a type of phlox that blooms very early in spring.

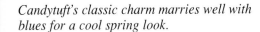

Candytuft's classic charm marries well with blues for a cool spring look.

55

Canna

Hybrid cannas come in a myriad of colors, including hues of the setting sun.

Tropical looking and flamboyant, canna is an easy-to-grow perennial that calls attention to the garden today just as it did years ago. From midsummer until the first frost, the flowers unfold red, orange, salmon, pink, or yellow like fluttering wings atop upright leafy stalks. The bold, upturned leaves may be emerald green, variegated, bronze, or purple, and attract plenty of attention on their own.

In the Landscape

Ranging in height from 1½ to 8 feet, there is a canna for every place you want to make a dramatic statement. Because of their large leaves, cannas have a strong, coarse texture in the landscape. In large spaces, they are perfect for massing at the end of a view across a lawn, a terrace, or other open area. Larger selections can even be used as summer screens. In smaller spaces, plant cannas in groups of three for bold texture in a flower border or next to a terrace or a sidewalk.

Avoid planting cannas in a single row; the plants appear fuller when planted in clumps of three or more. You can also mass the plants for a sweeping curve or a large, coarse textural change in a perennial border. To achieve a solid look, space them 12 to 18 inches apart, depending on their mature size.

A mass of cannas is most impressive when viewed across a lawn, a terrace, or another open area.

Cannas are also bold enough to stand alone as accents in a small courtyard or a corner of a patio. They are ideal for using around water features, such as pools, ponds, or bird baths.

Dwarf selections are popular for containers, as they remain small and will not topple. Although cannas are generally cold hardy only through Zone 7, growing them in containers is one way to extend their range northward; pots may be moved into a basement or a garage for winter.

AT A GLANCE

❖

CANNA

Canna x *generalis*

Features: tropical blooms; coarse foliage

Colors: red, orange, salmon, pink, yellow

Height: 1½ to 8 feet

Light: full sun

Soil: rich, well drained

Water: high

Pests: canna leaf roller

Native: no

Range: Zones 7 to 10

Remarks: tolerates soggy soil

Different Selections

Most of the cannas for sale today are the result of centuries of breeding. Old selections such as The President, a tried-and-true red, are still very popular. The Pfitzer dwarfs grow 1½ to 2 feet tall and include the brilliant Chinese Coral and Crimson Beauty. Pink President is a lovely green-leafed canna that grows about 3 feet tall. Wyoming is a striking combination of bronze leaves and red-orange blooms that tops 4 feet. Conestoga features lemon yellow flowers and is 5 to 6 feet tall. Tropical Rose is an All-America Selections winner that is easy to grow from seed (unlike most hybrid cannas). It grows 2 to 3 feet tall.

Planting and Care

Plant cannas in full sun in spring once the danger of frost has passed; set rhizomes 3 to 4 inches deep. As soon as the weather warms, the rhizomes will sprout, sending leaves up very quickly. The first blooms appear by early summer. Plants set out as late as July will have plenty of time to bloom for a late-summer and early-fall show. Although rich, moist soil is their preference, they will grow in either sandy or clay soil. They do not mind wet conditions and can easily grow beside a sunny stream, where they may grow taller than in a garden.

Cut off blossoms after they fade to prolong flowering. Be careful not to cut off any flowering shoots that may be coming out just below the spent blossoms. On established clumps, remove the entire flower stem, leaves and all, once its blossoms are spent; cut back to just above ground level. This thins the clump and permits light to reach any newly developing flower stems. You can also encourage more blooms by feeding with a liquid bloom-boosting plant food every few weeks from spring to fall.

Rejuvenate crowded plants by digging and separating them after the first frost in fall. Discard old rhizomes, saving the younger ones that have eyes. In areas where cannas are not cold hardy, you may store the rhizomes for winter in a room where the temperature stays above freezing. Pack them in peat moss or vermiculite.

Troubleshooting

Be prepared to combat the canna leaf roller, a caterpillar that rolls itself in the new leaves, chewing holes in them; these holes appear as the leaves unfold from the center of the plant. Spray at the first sign of infestation or pick the caterpillars from the plants.

Tropical Rose is an All-America Selections winner that can be grown from seed.

Cardinal Flower

Expect vivid red blossoms and hummingbirds when you plant cardinal flower.

The blossoms of cardinal flower offer the deepest, truest reds of nature. Indeed, this plant's jewel-toned tiara will make you stop and pause if you happen upon it near a stream in the woods or a wet meadow where it grows wild.

Yet despite their bold color, the blossoms of cardinal flower are delicate, gradually opening from bottom to top with spikes on 2- to 4-foot-tall upright stalks. These progressive blooms make the show long lasting. Although the blossoms first appear in midsummer, the ones at the tip of the stalk are often still in bloom during autumn.

Cardinal flower is native throughout the South, flowering and reseeding in low areas, near standing water, and along the banks of streams. It prefers moist soil in the garden as well. While thriving in situations in which many other perennials would rot, cardinal flower can also tolerate dry soil.

In the Landscape

Cardinal flower is at its best in a landscape setting similar to its native habitat—beside a partially shaded stream or pool. It likes wet soil. A group of cardinal flowers is perfect when planted against the lush green of ferns or hostas in a woodland garden or paired with other native plants, such as a white spider lily. Cardinal flower also works well in a flower border, where it offers both strong vertical effect and enduring summer color. For some excitement in a border, try contrasting

In a setting similar to the stream banks that are their native habitat, cardinal flowers create a display that begins in midsummer and can last until fall.

AT A GLANCE
❖
CARDINAL FLOWER
Lobelia cardinalis

Features: dozens of flowers on tall spikes in midsummer and fall

Colors: red, blue

Height: 2 to 4 feet

Light: filtered sun or light shade

Soil: rich, moist

Water: medium to high

Pests: none specific

Native: yes

Range: Zones 2 to 9

Remarks: prized for long blooming time in late summer

cardinal flower with deep purple or white Louisiana iris, which also likes wet soil. Wherever you grow cardinal flower, count on visits from hummingbirds, for they relish the blossoms' nectar.

Species and Selections

Native cardinal flower is often sold simply as *Lobelia cardinalis*. However, several selections are also available, including interesting red-leafed forms such as Bees Flame and Queen Victoria.

Azure sage *(Lobelia siphilitica)* is a species prized for the brilliant deep blue of its blossoms. It also blooms in fall, making a spiked blue complement to goldenrod, aster, and other fall-flowering perennials.

The hybrid *Lobelia* x *vedrariensis* is an unusual purple-flowered plant that blooms from summer to fall. It has very full flower spikes that appear atop 3-foot stems and are prized for cutting.

Cardinal flowers are a striking way to add seasonal color to a border.

Planting and Care

Cardinal flowers grow best in filtered light. As with most perennials, however, the farther south you live, the more shade the plants will need. If you do not have enough shade in your garden, make sure the plants get plenty of moisture, even during winter. From Zone 5 northward, cardinal flower will do well in full sun.

Prepare the soil for cardinal flowers by incorporating a generous amount of sphagnum peat moss, compost, manure, or other organic material into your garden soil. Mulch around the plants to conserve moisture but be careful not to cover the foliage as it may rot during a wet winter.

The native, unhybridized cardinal flower reseeds. Transplant young plants into other garden areas or let them grow where they appear. Cardinal flowers may only last for a season or two in some gardens. For insurance, save seeds or divide plants in fall for the first few years until you see how they perform in your garden.

Catmint

AT A GLANCE

❖

CATMINT
Nepeta species

Features: blue or lavender spikes with gray-green foliage

Colors: dark purple, lavender, white

Height: 12 to 36 inches

Light: full sun to partial shade

Soil: rich, well drained

Water: medium

Pests: none specific

Native: no

Range: Zones 3 to 9

Remarks: for edgings, borders, mass plantings

Catmint wears a cloak of scented blue to lavender flowers from late spring through early summer. Then, when many other early-flowering perennials let you down, these heat-tolerant plants begin spreading as a handsome mound of gray-green foliage. Catmint is a relative of the feline favorite, catnip, but does not have the same intoxicating effect on cats.

In the Landscape

Related to the sages, catmints have been a traditional part of the herb garden and have long been popular in Europe. In this country, however, they are prized for the front of a sunny flower border; there are several popular species and selections. Growing 12 to 18 inches tall, catmints make lovely edging plants. Because they will tolerate drier conditions, they are also a good choice for containers. Plant alone or in combination with other gray-leafed plants, such as lamb's-ears, bearded iris, or snow-in-summer. Large selections brighten the back of the border, especially when combined with yellow or pink yarrow or daisies.

Species and Selections

Persian catmint *(Nepeta mussinii)* is a seedling plant that is quite lovely, with small blue or white blooms and scented leaves. Because of variability among seedlings, dividing the original plant is recommended to preserve improved selections of the species, such as Blue Wonder, Blue Dwarf, and White Wonder. If cut back after it blooms, Persian catmint will flower again in the fall.

Faassen's catmint *(Nepeta* x *faassenii)* is a sterile hybrid, so it must be propagated by division or cuttings. A good ground cover or edging plant, it is long flowering but begins blooming slightly later than Persian catmint. Small, profuse lavender-blue blooms appear on upright stalks from early to midsummer and then sporadically through fall. The bloom stems are a bit stiffer than those of Persian catmint and stand up better in a hard rain. They also give the plant a more upright appearance.

You will also see named selections of catmint. Dropmore Hybrid is larger and showier than Persian or Faassen's catmint. Six Hills Giant grows to about 3 feet tall and equally wide.

Planting and Care

If properly cared for, catmint will continue to bloom from time to time through summer and into fall. Trim off the stem tips as the flowers fade.

Catmint is an ideal choice for the front of a flower bed. It creeps over the edge with flower-laden branches.

This summer pruning helps keep the plant tidy and compact; left unpruned, some of the lower leaves will turn brown, and the faded flower heads leave the plant looking untidy.

Choose a location that is sunny and well drained. Plants welcome afternoon shade in the lower and coastal South. Although fertilizer will probably not be necessary unless your soil is extremely sandy, catmint will appreciate the addition of organic matter. Organic matter, along with a slightly raised bed, will also improve drainage. Good drainage is essential, especially during the winter when soggy soil can kill the plant.

The habit of catmint is to spread slowly but not too vigorously. You will probably need to divide the clump every two to three years. This is an opportunity to transplant cuttings to other areas of the garden or to share them with gardening friends.

Chrysanthemum

This blossom is typical of the fall shades for which mums are revered.

AT A GLANCE
❖
CHRYSANTHEMUM
Dendranthema grandiflora

Features: mounds of colorful
   flowers
Colors: white, yellow, bronze,
   red, lavender, pink
Height: 1 to 3 feet
Light: full sun
Soil: light, well drained
Water: medium
Pests: aphids, whiteflies,
   spider mites
Native: no
Range: Zones 5 to 9
Remarks: ideal for fall flower
   borders and containers

Although native to China and Japan, chrysanthemums have become an American symbol of fall that may be seen everywhere from roadside stands and garden shops to grocery stores and even flea markets. Mums offer a variety of flower colors, sizes, and shapes for the garden and for cutting to bring indoors.

You may remember mums as "grandma's flowers," sprawling over flower beds and covered with pink, white, or yellow blooms until October, when they stand up to the first light frost. Thanks to the work of plant breeders, today's mums are more compact, bloom more heavily, and have longer lasting flowers than their predecessors. Many bloom quite early, stretching the season from midsummer to late fall.

In the Landscape

These favorites are usually found for sale in full bloom in the fall, ready to be planted for instant color in flower beds and pots. You can create a sensation with only a few mums by mixing them with existing plants. Pair yellow mums with sedum Autumn Joy, purple aster, or Mexican bush sage. Mix lavender selections with gray lamb's-ear, artemisia Silver King, or bright yellow goldenrod. You can also tuck in a few to enliven a bed of annuals at the end of the season.

Mums are also ideal for brightening dim areas of the garden or adding a spark of color to attract attention.

At home in a large clay pot, popular Yellow Jacket mums pick up the light from taller goldenrods and make this fall border sing. At the front of the border, other mums are tucked into the bed to blend with sedum, narrowleaf zinnia, lamb's-ear, and marigolds.

A single planter with two or three mums is enough to brighten an entry.

Placing them in front of a dark background, such as evergreens or a stone wall, will increase the visibility of the blooms.

Try using them in attractive containers along a sidewalk, near garden steps, or beside an entry. If you only have room for one or two mums, put them in an attractive planter for your porch, terrace, or deck—the cheerful blossoms will last for weeks.

Different Selections

Chrysanthemums have been bred extensively; there are many different named selections, although the mums in garden centers are rarely named, sold instead by color, shape, and size of bloom. You will also find very compact, small-flowered "garden mums," which are so named because they withstand rain and garden conditions better than the larger flowered types.

Whatever mums you buy, you will find that many will bloom much earlier or later in years following the season in which you plant them. This is because hybrid mums produced in a greenhouse are often timed to bloom at a specific time, in order to appear attractive to shoppers.

Growers in your area are generally aware of the mums that do well there, so whatever is for sale at your local garden center is likely to be well adapted to your climate. Check to make sure plants are not rootbound when you buy them in the fall. If so, be sure to spread out the roots before planting. (Turn to page 22 to read about dealing with rootbound transplants.) You can transplant "hospital room" mums outdoors, but they will not perform nearly as well as those bred for the garden.

A mass of chrysanthemums will last about a month in the cool fall weather. You can often extend the blooming for another few weeks by pinching off the old blooms.

Daisylike white mums bring a springtime freshness to the fall landscape.

Planting and Care

You can keep many mums blooming longer by pinching the old blooms as soon as they fade. This is especially successful in the lower and coastal South, where fall is very long and mild.

If you have kept your mums in pots, you may plant them in the garden after they have bloomed. Following a hard freeze, cut the top growth back to the ground and cover the plants with a 2- to 3-inch layer of pine straw or shredded bark. However, if you live in the upper South or farther north, it is best to plant mums outdoors in the spring.

To keep plants disease free, many gardeners dig their mums up every spring and plant new plants, either by separating and replanting new shoots or by taking cuttings. Mums are very easy to root. Put cuttings in potting mix, water regularly (but not too heavily), and in about a month, you will have new plants to set out. Mums need a lot of plant food; fertilize with a balanced fertilizer in March, May, and July.

While not finicky, mums require extra maintenance to retain a bushy, mounding form. Using garden shears, cut plants back by one-third in May and late July so they will not fall over when they bloom in fall. Once flowers are nipped by heavy frost, cut plants back for the winter.

Troubleshooting

Aphids, whiteflies, and spider mites may bother mums. Turn to pages 124 to 125 for more about these pests.

Coneflower

Although a wildflower, orange coneflower looks nice in garden settings, too. This is the selection Goldsturm.

Whether growing wild along a roadside or sitting pretty in a flower garden, native coneflowers attract attention. Their colorful, daisylike flowers thrive without pampering from June through the first frost, putting on their best show in midsummer when other flowers are waning. Most coneflowers grow 2 to 3 feet tall and have dark green, coarse foliage; they make fine border plants with little or no coaxing. There are two main types: orange coneflowers and purple coneflowers. Both are easy to grow and make long-lasting cut flowers.

In the Landscape

Because coneflowers are wildflowers, you can mass them along the periphery of a wooded area or use them in clumps in sunny parts of a naturalistic landscape. They are particularly at home in settings where weathered wood and split-rail fences are part of the garden. They also mix beautifully in a flower border beside a terrace or near an entry. Coneflower's tall, erect form and unaffected beauty make it a graceful cut flower. And in the fall, goldfinches dine on the plentiful seed of purple coneflowers.

Species and Selections

Orange coneflowers are actually more yellow than orange. Goldsturm is the most popular selection. Its vivid color and open form make it a versatile addition to the garden. Plant it with other perennials or alone in a large mass for fresh, bright color in late summer, when other blossoms tend to look tired. A profusely flowering plant, Goldsturm is a 2- to 3-foot-tall plant with golden yellow blossoms that are 3 to 4 inches in diameter. Since this coneflower spreads by rhizomes, a planting of Goldsturm will slowly increase in size over the years, so give it plenty of room.

AT A GLANCE
❖
ORANGE CONEFLOWER
Rudbeckia fulgida

Features: daisylike summer blooms

Colors: golden yellow with brown centers

Height: 1½ to 3 feet

Light: full sun to partial shade

Soil: poor to average

Water: medium

Pests: none specific

Native: yes

Range: Zones 3 to 9

Remarks: low-maintenance plants, good for beginners

Coreopsis

Bigflower coreopsis is so named because its blooms are larger than those of other coreopsis species.

Gardeners who design flower borders in sedate pinks, blues, and whites often look to the excitement of yellow coreopsis for panache. These daisylike Southern natives are not only lively and pretty, but they are tolerant of drought, are bothered by no pests, and beg only an occasional feeding. To top it off, your strategic choice among the different species of coreopsis, also called tickseed, will yield an ongoing show of bright yellow blooms in succession from April through September. For those who like the form and hardy nature of coreopsis but prefer quieter color schemes, threadleaf coreopsis offers smaller blooms, finer foliage, and pale yellow or pink flowers that add a fresh new look to the garden.

In the Landscape

The eye is drawn to yellow, so take advantage of this when planting coreopsis in your garden. Use coreopsis to brighten an area, establish a focal point, or draw attention from a distance. While coreopsis blends well with reds, oranges, and other warm colors, you can pair it with a cool blue, lavender, or purple as well. Suitable blue companions include mealycup sage, Mexican bush sage, purple verbena, ageratum, and blue larkspur. The bright yellow or gold blooms of coreopsis bring blues to life.

Most species of coreopsis are well suited to flower beds that do not get much pampering, such as those that are exposed to heat near

Coreopsis breathes excitement into borders dominated by tame shades of pink, purple, and white.

a driveway and the street. They are flexible enough to grow in moist or dry conditions and work well as a ground cover in naturalistic landscapes.

Species and Selections

Dwarf-eared coreopsis (*Coreopsis auriculata* Nana) is the first coreopsis to bloom each year. Dwarf-eared coreopsis gets its name from the small lobes on its leaves that stick out like ears. Though not as widely planted as other species, it has delightful flowers and a neat habit. Growing only 2 to 4 inches tall, it forms a slowly spreading mat of ground cover and will also poke its way through cracks in rocks. From early spring to the beginning of summer it produces golden flowers that are up to 2 inches across and appear atop wiry, 8- to 10-inch stems. Dwarf-eared coreopsis, with its dark green foliage, makes a fine edging plant or addition to the front of a border.

Dwarf-eared coreopsis runs along the surface of a woodland garden in spring.

Bigflower coreopsis *(Coreopsis grandiflora)* is a short-lived perennial that grows up to 3 feet tall. Bigflower coreopsis bears 3-inch blossoms on long stems, making it perfect for cutting. It begins blooming in early summer and continues until fall. Mayfield Giant is the most popular selection, coming back each year from seed. This is a great filler plant for sunny borders or mass plantings and is a perfect addition to a wildflower garden.

In the wild, bigflower coreopsis often takes a year to begin blooming and tends to flop during rainy weather. For better performance, try Early Sunrise, an All-America Selections winner that is shorter and stockier than the species, growing only 18 inches tall. It bears semidouble blooms and is longer lived; this perennial blooms from seed the first year. Another dwarf selection, Goldfink, grows about 10 inches tall and performs admirably in the front of a border. Sunray, a medium-sized plant, grows to about 2 feet tall and is more heat tolerant; it is better suited to the coastal South. Sunray features bright yellow double blossoms on tall stems, which make striking cut flowers.

Lanceleaf coreopsis *(Coreopsis lanceolata)* looks much like bigflower coreopsis. Lanceleaf coreopsis is a little shorter, less leafy, and bears slightly fewer flowers, but its life span is longer. Like bigflower coreopsis, this plant tends to droop in the rain. Brown Eyes is a selection with single yellow flowers that have a maroon band encircling the center.

Lanceleaf coreopsis offers a bold splash of color in the garden all summer long.

Noted for its finely dissected foliage, threadleaf coreopsis is the most drought-tolerant species.

Threadleaf coreopsis *(Coreopsis verticillata)* is probably the toughest and most drought tolerant of all species of coreopsis. Named for its fernlike, finely dissected foliage, it is **stoloniferous,** spreading underground to form ever-widening clumps, and blooms the entire summer. The most popular selection, Golden Showers, forms 18-inch to 2-foot mounds of buttercup-yellow blossoms. Zagreb, a dwarf form, grows about 18 inches tall with deep yellow flowers. Gardeners also love Moonbeam, with blooms of pale yellow and other soft shades.

Pink tickseed *(Coreopsis rosea)* has the same growth habit and fine foliage as threadleaf coreopsis but offers a new color palette—rosy blooms with bright yellow centers. It prefers moist soil and is well suited to sunny areas near water. Group two or three plants together for a showy clump. Or plant pink tickseed in a container, such as a hanging basket, for an airy show of blooms.

Plains coreopsis *(Coreopsis tinctoria)* is an annual that should not be confused with its perennial cousins.

Planting and Care

You may plant coreopsis in full sun to partial shade, depending upon the selection. It prefers soil that is poor but well drained. Avoid poorly drained, heavy clay; if planting in heavy soil, raise the level of the bed to provide good drainage. Feed only once in late winter or early spring with a slow-release flower food. Be sure to remove spent flowers during the blooming season to prolong flowering and keep plants neat and healthy.

Save seed from bigflower coreopsis and divide other species of coreopsis in spring or fall every two years.

Daisy

Daisies are perhaps the most familiar of all flowers, cheerfully bobbing in gardens around the country. Although many flowering plants are called daisies, one genus, *Chrysanthemum,* contains many of the best-known and most dependable daisies. Botanically, a daisy is a composite flower with a well-defined center and a skirt of ray flowers that are the petals of the bloom.

These flowers have a simple appeal that marries well with stronger, brighter flowers in beds and borders. Their flat, round blooms contrast nicely with the upright vertical spikes of salvia or larkspur, and the daisies' yellow centers come to life when mixed with yellow pansies.

In the Landscape

By planting several types of daisies, you can have a succession of blooms from spring until fall. Taller daisies are effective when grouped near the middle or back of a mixed flower border, where they break up competing colors with their sunny white blooms. Because they are tough, they are good to use when naturalizing a wildflower garden, a meadow, or an area that receives little attention. They make classic mailbox plantings and work well along picket or split-rail fences. Because the blooms are so prolific, you can enjoy as many bouquets of cut flowers as you choose to cut.

Species and Selections

Shasta daisy *(Chrysanthemum* x *superbum)* is probably the best-known daisy. Shasta daisy blooms in late spring and early summer. It is available with single or double flowers and ranges in height from 15 to 30 inches. The foliage is deep green and is evergreen in the lower and coastal South. Aglaya and Diener's Double offer tall, double flowers, while Miss Muffet is a single-flowered dwarf selection. Polaris is single-flowered with 5-inch blooms. Alaska is named for its

The yellow centers of Shasta daisies are a perfect match for deep yellow pansies.

Daisies are excellent cut flowers.

AT A GLANCE

DAISY

Chrysanthemum species and hybrids

Features: white blooms with yellow centers from spring to summer

Colors: white, pink, or yellow

Height: 8 inches to 2½ feet

Light: full sun

Soil: moderately fertile, well drained

Water: medium

Pests: none specific

Native: no

Range: Zones 4 to 9

Remarks: old-fashioned, cheerful perennials

Sturdy perennials, Shasta daisies highlight a sunny border.

extreme cold hardiness, growing to Zone 3; it has 3-inch flowers on 3-foot-tall stems. Wirral Pride's flowers have short, wide petals. Shasta daisies form large clumps and live from two to three years, so divide them every other year. For the best performance in the lower South, choose compact, early-blooming selections as Shasta daisies suffer in the heat and humidity of summer. The length of their blooming season depends upon the selection you choose, area weather, and your faithfulness in removing the faded blossoms.

Oxeye daisy *(Chrysanthemum leucanthemum)* is the earliest blooming daisy. Its white blooms continue for two to three months, from early to late spring. Oxeye daisy prefers average soil; in richer conditions, it is apt to require staking. A prolific reseeder, oxeye daisy is easy to dig and give away. Fall is the best time to dig seedlings or to divide the parent plant. An improved selection named May Queen offers sturdier stems and is less likely to reseed. The more blooms you pick, the more you get.

Feverfew *(Chrysanthemum parthenium)* is an old favorite. These aromatic yellow daisies are tiny and plentiful, and their blooms will continue all summer if you keep cutting them. Reaching 1 to 2 feet tall, they are ideal for summer arrangements. The single-flowering feverfew is a prolific reseeder; flore-pleno is a double-flowered selection. Pinch back plants if they grow out of control.

Nippon daisy *(Chrysanthemum nipponicum)* is a 2-foot-tall plant that blooms in autumn. These stems, unlike those of other daisies, are woody and bear coarse, stiff foliage. The result is foliage interest all summer and white blossoms in fall.

Clara Curtis *(Chrysanthemum* x *rubellum)* is a hybrid chrysanthemum that bears stunning pink blooms with yellow centers. It blooms in the summer and continues through fall if you remove the faded blooms. Plants grow 2 to 3 feet tall.

Planting and Care

Daisies will thrive in full sun or light shade. Moderately fertile, well-drained soil is ideal. Daisies need moisture for strong growth and long-lasting flowers, especially during the hottest part of the summer. Cut back plants after they bloom to keep them tidy. Even when not in bloom, their attractive green rosettes make an attractive ground cover.

Seedlings that appear in summer may not survive the heat; those that sprout in fall can be transplanted within the garden.

Daylily

Daylilies have been called the lazy gardener's flower because few perennials give so much for so little. But this depends on which daylily you choose. Of the hundreds of selections, some are grown strictly for their outstanding, prize-winning flowers, while others are perfect for durability in the landscape. If you choose your daylilies carefully, it is possible to enjoy them six to ten months of the year.

Thanks to plant breeders, daylilies are no longer limited to the tawny daylily, the well-known tall plant with orange blooms that is found along roadsides and at many old homesites. Today's hybrids come in nearly every color—cream, yellow, orange, apricot, pink, lavender, red, near-black, and bicolors. Even when daylilies are not in bloom, the fan-shaped foliage of many selections lends its green, grassy, curving lines to the landscape. And once they have put their hardy roots down in well-drained soil, the toughest selections require very little care, only occasional division.

Although the bloom lasts only a day, each *scape* (flowering stalk) has several flower buds that bloom in succession.

In the Landscape

Daylilies are classics in a cottage garden when planted in drifts in a border of mixed flowers or shrubs. Tall selections (36 inches) work best at the back of the border or against a wall or a fence. Combine them with other tall perennials, such as phlox, boltonia, New England asters, or daisies. Lower growing selections (16 to 36 inches) add impact when planted in neat clumps and are often used in foundation plantings. Daffodils and daylilies are ideal companions;

Few flowers rival daylilies for giving so much beauty from so little attention.

AT A GLANCE
❖
DAYLILY
Hemerocallis species and hybrids

Features: showy blooms, grassy foliage

Colors: yellow, orange, pink, mauve, red, purple

Height: 8 inches to 3 feet

Light: full sun to partial shade

Soil: well drained

Water: medium

Pests: aphids, spider mites, slugs, nematodes, thrips

Native: no

Range: Zones 3 to 10

Remarks: easy summer color, good for ground cover

Lemon-yellow daylilies light up the summer garden when planted in masses against the backdrop of perennials and shrubs.

Daylilies spread rapidly, bloom repeatedly, and are good ground cover.

Old-fashioned favorites, daylilies make themselves at home with other wildflowers in cottage or country gardens.

the daffodils bloom first, and then the daylily foliage comes up to hide the daffodil foliage as it begins to yellow.

Daylilies are also popular for mass planting, and many of the tougher selections will spread dependably to naturalize an area or to form a stable ground cover. Because their roots help stabilize the soil, daylilies are effective ground covers on steep slopes in full sun. Compact selections (8 to 16 inches) work well in containers on decks and patios or used for spots of color near stairs, doorways, or garden features. Select fragrant daylilies to plant near a favorite outdoor sitting area.

Species and Selections

The most difficult part of gardening with daylilies is choosing the right plant for your needs. Local daylily societies can usually tell you which ones grow best in your area. Daylilies are bred for different purposes; each selection is derived from different parent plants, so one daylily is better suited to a cold climate than another, for example. Generally, dormant daylilies require some cold weather, while evergreen types do better in the South. But there are exceptions to this rule—another reason to inquire locally.

Many of the beautiful blooms you see in catalogs come from selections that require more pampering and are grown strictly for the flower. Typically, such daylilies are in bloom for only three weeks, while tougher landscape selections bloom for much longer. If you are looking for exquisite large blooms in unusual colors to fit a spot in a perennial border, look to the fancier hybrids; keep in mind that they will need a bit more fertilizer and water than the tough landscape daylilies that you can plant and almost forget once they are established.

Tawny daylily *(Hemerocallis fulva)*, a dusty orange daylily naturalized throughout the South, is the one you probably remember from your grandmother's garden. It works well in a cottage garden or a wildflower setting and is very tough. Most gardeners will be happy to share theirs with you, so ask around before you buy. Tawny daylily is very tall with scapes up to 4 feet tall when in bloom. It blooms for two to three weeks in early to midsummer.

Lemon lily *(Hemerocallis lilio-asphodelus)* is also known as *Hemerocallis flava* and is another beloved, old-fashioned daylily. It features pale yellow blooms atop 3-foot scapes, and has a delicate lemon fragrance, is long lasting, and spreads rapidly. Pair it with blue or white blooms, or use it in a mass planting by itself.

Reblooming daylilies *(Hemerocallis hybrids)* are a group of hybrids that are bred for their ability to rebloom through the warm months. Also included are the rugged landscape daylilies, so called for their durability, ability to multiply, and their longer season of bloom. Stella de Oro has set the standard for reblooming landscape daylilies, winning points for its flushes of golden yellow flowers from late spring through fall, provided it is not stressed by drought. However, it does not rebloom dependably in Zones 8, 9, and 10. This selection is compact, about 24 inches tall, and will grow in a container. Happy Returns, a new hybrid of Stella de Oro, is even smaller (15 to 18 inches) with a more lemon yellow flower and the same long bloom time.

Black-eyed Stella is a golden yellow reblooming daylily noted for its maroon eye, a departure from the standard landscape daylily, which is typically solid orange to yellow. Black-eyed Stella has surpassed Stella de Oro in its ability to produce many blossoms in hot climates. When given adequate water and fertilizer to supply nutrients for an extralong growing season, it will bloom for eight or nine months in Zones 9 and 10. It is also hardy enough to grow in the

It is hard to beat daylilies for bold summer colors like this pure red, which breeders have worked hard to capture.

Tawny daylily, which grows naturally throughout the South, can look quite elegant in a formal planting.

Carol Colossal is a spidery yellow daylily.

same cold climates as Stella de Oro and will bloom for the duration of the warm season.

Other popular reblooming hybrids include Bitsy, a dwarf yellow, Green Glitter, a tall yellow with a green throat, and Becky Lynn, prized for rose-colored blooms atop 2-foot-tall stalks. When choosing daylilies for ground cover, you will want to select those that multiply rapidly and vigorously. Some rebloomers also spread quite rapidly; they include Aztec Gold, with thin golden petals, Nashville Star, with thin, red petals, and Irish Elf, with lemon-yellow blooms on 18-inch scapes. Black-eyed Stella also multiplies quickly.

Fancy daylilies *(Hemerocallis hybrids)* are the hybrids for perennial borders and for showy displays. This group includes the majority of hybrid daylilies that have been bred by daylily fanciers for color and form. Read catalog descriptions carefully and check with your local daylily society before you buy to be sure that the one you are considering is adapted to your climate.

Planting and Care

Daylilies like well-drained soil with plenty of organic matter, but they will flourish in sandy or clay soils. Good drainage is the only absolute requirement. A raised bed is one easy way to accomplish this. Full sun produces the maximum number of blooms, but daylilies will also perform well in partial shade. In fact, deep red and purple selections need protection from the afternoon sun.

The daylily show in summer features a concert of color, form, and size.

Disco Rose has a unique color combination.

While daylilies do fine with little fuss, you will have larger, more profuse flowers if you pamper them. Each fall, improve the soil by working in good topsoil along with compost and leaf mold. Fertilize in early March and again several weeks later with cottonseed meal, alfalfa meal, or a slow-release chemical fertilizer to improve the soil and release nutrients slowly. Then, as plants begin to bud, sprinkle ¼ cup of slow-release flower food around the plants; this extra nitrogen results in larger flowers and more vivid colors.

To keep daylilies looking neat, remove the spent blooms from the day before. Many gardeners also clean up decaying foliage and cut scapes back once they have ceased blooming in order to conserve the plants' energy.

During summer droughts when plants are blooming, give them plenty of water. Every couple of years, divide daylilies in the fall and create new beds or share them with friends. You can dig plants and divide them at any time, provided the ground is not cold or frozen. It is best not to move them in July or August when it is quite hot. Ideal times for planting and transplanting are early to midspring and early to midfall.

Troubleshooting

Daylilies are remarkably trouble free. But when pests do strike, they can be deadly. Watch out for aphids, spider mites, and slugs. Turn to pages 124 to 125 for more about these pests. Nematodes and thrips may also be problems.

Although each flower lasts only a day, each scape features subsequent blooms in rapid succession, which continue the color.

Dianthus

The popular Bath's Pink features a dark eye in the center of a toothed blossom.

Dianthus is a family of classic cottage-garden flowers that includes both new hybrids and old favorites. These perennials are also called pinks because they look like an airy drift of pink. If you match the right selection with the right spot, you will enjoy spring, summer, and fall blooms in candied colors that also include red, white, purple, and bicolors as well as evergreen foliage.

Dianthus are actually hardy cousins of the carnation; both are fragrant and have delicate, toothed petals. But dianthus blooms are smaller, 1 to 2 inches in diameter, and may be either single or double. Dianthus prefers a sunny, well-drained location and is undaunted by a dry summer. However, it may fall victim to stem rot in warm, rainy weather, and gardeners in coastal areas may have difficulty growing most types.

In the Landscape

Use dianthus at the front of a flower border or to spill over the edge of a pot or rock wall. A few widely spaced transplants will grow into a carpet of foliage. During winter, the hardy foliage of gray-leafed dianthus appears quite blue, contrasting against the subdued shades of the season. Low-growing selections are excellent ground covers and can be trimmed back after they bloom so that the planting remains thick. Cascading dianthus looks good in hanging baskets. Evergreen dianthus is an asset in a rock garden.

Species and Selections

If you are looking for dependable dianthus, there are several species and selections you can usually count on for your garden. The more than 200 species of *Dianthus* include annual, biennial, and perennial selections. The annual *Dianthus chinensis* is what you see every

---

AT A GLANCE
❖
DIANTHUS
Dianthus species

Features: clouds of carnation-like flowers in spring, summer, and fall

Colors: pink, salmon, purple, red, white

Height: 3 inches to 2 feet

Light: full or at least a half day's sun

Soil: well drained, neutral

Water: medium

Pests: none specific

Native: no

Range: Zones 4 to 8

Remarks: handsome, fine-textured, evergreen foliage

spring in cell packs at the garden center. These are tough, pretty plants, some of which overwinter in Zones 7 and farther south, but they are not reliably perennial or evergreen. Another old-fashioned dianthus is the biennial sweet William, *Dianthus barbatus*. If planted in the fall, it will reward you with stunning blooms the following May.

For perennial dianthus, look for some of the following selections:

Cottage pink *(Dianthus plumarius)* is both heat and drought tolerant. The foliage grows into a mat of blue-gray leaves that is just as attractive as the flowers. In late spring, cottage pinks are transformed into a cloud of sweetly fragrant little flowers. As the blossoms fade, pinch them off to keep the plant tidy.

Allwood hybrids *(Dianthus* x *allwoodii)* bloom repeatedly through the summer and are long-lived. On a sunny day you can smell their fragrance in the air.

Even when not in bloom, dianthus makes an excellent evergreen ground cover.

Cottage pinks encircle a sundial to form the focal point of this herb garden.

Gaura

The delicate, mothlike flowers and pink buds of gaura show off all summer long.

Gaura, a pretty, native perennial, is not flashy but its faithful sprays of small, white flowers win the respect of most gardeners. Although native to the prairies of Texas and Louisiana, it is perfectly adapted to gardens throughout the South, even the coldest extremes of the upper South.

Gaura's long, reddish stems bear delicate pink buds that open into moth-shaped white flowers, which come and go for five or six months from midspring until the first frost. In a flower border, the blooms hover above and between more dense clumps of flowers in a snowy mass. A stalwart resistance to heat and humidity means continuous bloom; the flowering stems lengthen to reach a height of 3 to 5 feet with the passing summer days.

In the Landscape

Gaura's delicate blooms are so charming when viewed up close that the plant is well placed near steps or a walkway. However, it is more frequently used as a filler in a flower border. Its long stems are an advantage in flower borders because they stand above the mass of summer flowers, such as daylilies, black-eyed Susans, and purple coneflowers. Its bushy form also creates sufficient mass to fill a void where spring flowers have died down.

Different Selections

Most often sold simply as gaura, few named selections or hybrids of the plant are available. However, there is a pink form.

Planting and Care

Gaura blooms best in full sun but will also perform in partial shade. It also likes well-drained soil. In fact, sandy soil is best; in rich organic soil, gaura grows too high to remain upright. Because it is deep rooted, gaura tolerates dry summers very well. Even so, it helps to deadhead most spent blossoms to keep the plant healthy and promote bloom throughout the season. In fact, some gardeners prefer to control the ultimate height with timely pruning. The first flush of bloom lasts about a month. In July, the plant can be cut back to approximately 18 inches. The second blooming period will be shorter and thicker than the first.

This taprooted perennial propagates by seedlings that spring up around the plant; these grow to flowering size after the first year. When you cut back gaura, leave one plant unpruned so that it will reseed. You should transplant seedlings while they are young, taking care not to sever the carrotlike root. Because of the deep roots, parent plants resist transplanting.

Gaura makes a strong statement in a mixed border, where it rises above other plants and creates clouds of white blossoms from May until the first frost.

Ginger Lily

The flowers of ginger lilies resemble pure white butterflies and release one of the most fragrant scents of summer.

Ginger lily has long been handed down from generation to generation—dug, divided, and planted for its fragrant late-summer blooms. Also known as butterfly ginger, the plant has upright tropical stalks of long, slender leaves. Like silken white butterflies, the blossoms cluster atop each stem, releasing a sweet fragrance rivaled only by gardenias. This scent seems to grow stronger late in the day and lingers in the evening air. Ginger lilies also last in cut arrangements. Indoors, their fragrance will have even greater impact, as will their lush green foliage.

In the Landscape

Ginger lilies are decidedly tropical, due to their large size, exquisite blooms, and heady fragrance. They grow up to 4 to 6 feet tall, so place them where their palm-like foliage will be most pleasing and their scented flowers most appreciated. They are attractive in a border or as a background planting or a screen. Because they like moisture, they may be planted on a bank near a pool of water. Or place them near a door, a walkway, or stairs to treat visitors to their display. Their large leaves and vertical stalks give them a distinct shape and texture that will attract the eye even when the plants are not in bloom. You can use a clump of ginger lilies alone or surround them with tall ferns for a fine contrast at their base.

Planting and Care

Ginger lilies enjoy moist soil that is rich in organic matter, and they thrive in full sun to partial shade. Fertilize in late winter or early spring to fuel new growth. Take extra care to water plants that grow in full sun, since the large, lush leaves lose much moisture in the sun.

These robust plants grow from underground rhizomes. In south Florida and Texas, where frosts are few, ginger lilies remain green year-round. However, even in the mildest climate you will need to cut away ragged stems to renew the plant.

Elsewhere, ginger lilies tolerate freezing temperatures as low as 15 degrees. They will die back to the ground and sprout new growth each spring. To help ensure survival, cut back the brown foliage after the first frost and apply several inches of mulch. Gardeners in the middle and upper South may want to dig their plants each year and store the rhizomes in the basement or garage as they would the rhizomes of dahlias and caladiums.

The stems of ginger lilies will reach 4 to 6 feet in height. Like cannas, they do not branch, and their leafy stems grow into a clump. You can propagate them by dividing the rhizomes every three to four years. This also ensures continued flowering.

The large leaves and spreading, upright stalks give ginger lilies a distinctly tropical appearance.

Goldenrod

Rough-leafed goldenrod is a native species that boasts slender flower clusters, giving the plant an airy, graceful look.

This airy, golden yellow wildflower is not the hay fever villain many people think it is. Instead, it is a sturdy native perennial that displays unusual late-summer garden color. In a garden, goldenrod grows to become fuller and often more showy and vigorous than its counterparts on the side of the road. Since it is native to some of the harshest areas in the South, goldenrods can take whatever the Southern summer dishes out and still emerge fresh and beautiful for a month or more of color. There are several species; it has been grown and hybridized for years by Europeans, who appreciate its hardiness and have developed many improved selections that are available in this country.

Goldenrod's blooms have long, sturdy stems and are very useful in flower arrangements. Cut flowers last more than a week in the vase.

In the Landscape

Goldenrod's bright color and ill-founded reputation as a roadside allergen will immediately draw the eye, so use it wherever you want to call attention. (The real allergen is ragweed, an anonymous-looking green flower that often blooms next to goldenrod on the roadside.)

Goldenrod's feathery plumes will provide interesting form and texture as well as color in the garden. The many species and selections vary in size from 2 to 6 feet, offering a wide choice for placement. It is versatile enough to use among wildflowers or in a more formal, cultivated garden border.

In a garden, goldenrod is a surprisingly handsome companion to other tall perennials, such as tatarian aster, phlox, deep blue

---

AT A GLANCE
❖
GOLDENROD
Solidago species

Features: bright plumes in late summer and fall

Colors: golden yellow

Height: 2 to 5 feet

Light: full sun

Soil: poor to average

Water: low

Pests: none specific

Native: yes

Range: Zones 4 to 9

Remarks: does not cause hay fever, colorful cut flower, heat tolerant

veronica, ageratum, or blue salvia. Or try setting the golden yellow flowers against the backdrop of deep green shrubs.

In a naturalistic landscape, goldenrod may simply be used in clumps along a fence or a long driveway to imitate natural placement in the wild. Be prepared to dig and divide many of the plants if you put them in a small space—they spread by underground stems.

Species and Selections

There are many goldenrod species native throughout the United States. The following are some of the most popular for gardens.

Goldenrod *(Solidago altissima)* spreads rapidly by underground stems, so it can become invasive in a flower border. However, it is ideal for a meadowlike setting along the edge of a country property.

Rough-leafed goldenrod *(Solidago rugosa)* has graceful starbursts of gold flowers clustered along slender stalks. At heights of up to 6 feet, this goldenrod can make quite a display. Plant it in either dry or moist soil. This species does not spread rapidly so it is a good choice for a tight spot in a border. Fireworks is a more compact selection, growing only 3 to 4 feet tall.

Seaside goldenrod *(Solidago sempervirens)* is native to coastal areas, where it grows in full sun in sand and along brackish marshes. However, it will also thrive in the clay soils of more inland regions. Plant seaside goldenrod at the back of your flower border since it will grow 5 to 6 feet tall. Its vigorous, spreading roots are helpful in retarding erosion at beach homes.

Dyersweed goldenrod *(Solidago nemoralis)* is a smaller species, growing about 3 feet tall. This goldenrod is especially good for hot, dry locations. Since it blooms in late summer, it should be planted with the late-flowering seaside and rough-leafed goldenrods for an extended season of bloom and a variation in plant heights.

Scepter goldenrod *(Solidago erecta)* is one of the tallest of the goldenrods, growing up to 5 feet. It boasts large, pyramidal flower clusters. Plant it in full sun and you will have majestic golden spires in fall.

Sweet goldenrod *(Solidago odora)* is a good choice for those who enjoy scented plants. It is not the flowers that are fragrant but the willowy leaves, which have an anise scent when crushed. Unlike other species, sweet goldenrod will grow in partial shade. It blooms in late summer and reaches a height of 2 to 4 feet.

An arching clump of seaside goldenrod fills the garden with yellow plumes that can reach 6 feet in height.

Goldenmosa, an improved selection, mixes with wild ageratum, blue salvia, and narrowleaf zinnia.

While goldenrod typically blooms and dies down to a rosette on the ground, shrub goldenrod (*Solidago pauciflosculosa*) is a woody shrub that is 2 to 4 feet tall. It grows from the lower South into Florida in sandy soil, bearing its flowers in July. Its evergreen leaves have a medium texture, making it an attractive addition to the garden year-round. However, when grown in rich soil, shrub goldenrod will be leggy and will lose its natural form.

Hybrid selections are crosses of native species with European species of goldenrods. They include Goldenmosa, a selection that grows 2 to 3 feet tall and blooms in August and September. Baby Gold is true to its name, reaching only 1 to 2 feet tall. Peter Pan and Cloth of Gold both bloom when 1½ feet tall. Some gardeners find that native species are more vigorous and better adapted to Southern gardens than the hybrids, so try these hybrids in limited numbers until you know how they perform in your garden.

Planting and Care

Plant goldenrod in full sun in well-drained soil. No extra watering or fertilizing is necessary.

The pyramidal flower cluster is typical of many types of goldenrod, a versatile perennial for the late-summer and fall garden.

After the flowers fade, cut the stalks back to the ground; you will have a tidy rosette of foliage. Most types of goldenrod are evergreen through the winter. The tall species can be pruned to be made more compact; in July, cut them back to half their height, and they will be 1 to 2 feet shorter when they bloom.

Hybrid goldenrods can be propagated by dividing the plants, as they multiply with underground stems. The unhybridized types can be started from seed as well as through division. Collect seeds in late fall and germinate them in warm, humid conditions (see page 31 for more about this technique).

Heliopsis

Incomparabilis, a selection of rough heliopsis, sports semidouble flowers that are excellent for cutting.

A native wildflower, heliopsis bears sunny, drought-tolerant blooms that resemble sunflowers *(Helianthus)* but are smaller, bushier, and often more suitable to a residential garden. A favorite of both beginning and experienced gardeners, heliopsis not only performs well but also multiplies, so one or two plants will go a long way. Its abundance also makes it an excellent cut flower, perfect for gathering in jars for deck parties and picnics.

Heliopsis takes its name from the Greek, meaning "resembling the sun." Given plenty of sun and a little water, it will brighten your landscape and your flower arrangements with brilliant orange-yellow flowers from June to September. Plants may range from 2 to 5 feet tall with flowers 2 to 3 inches across, in singles or doubles, depending on the selection.

In the Landscape

Because of its long blooming season and modest demands, heliopsis should be a mainstay of the summer garden. Try the taller, lankier native version in a meadow, along a fence, or in a sunny wildflower bed. Plant newer, more compact hybrids in a perennial border. The height of heliopsis makes it suitable for the middle or rear of the bed. The vibrant blossoms combine well with salvia, phlox, Shasta daisies, purple coneflowers, pink daylilies, and ornamental grasses. Even when not in bloom, its deep green foliage is a nice contrast to silver-leafed plants, such as lamb's-ears, artemisia, and dusty miller.

Species and Selections

Sunflower heliopsis *(Heliopsis helianthoides)* is a native American species that is found wild from New York to Georgia. Growing 3 to 5 feet tall with a lax spreading habit, it bears single yellow flowers that are 2 to 3 inches across. Its leaves are dark green and have prominently toothed edges. Its natural, unkempt form makes it perfect for country, cottage, or native gardens.

Rough heliopsis *(Heliopsis scabra)* has leaves that are coarser and firmer than those of sunflower heliopsis. Because of its smaller, more compact shape and its larger flowers, rough heliopsis is the more popular of the two. Hybrid selections include Golden Plume, with golden double flowers, and two selections with yellow semidouble blooms, Incomparabilis and Summer Sun.

Planting and Care

Heliopsis grows well in all areas of the South except in south Florida. It adapts to many soils but does best in well-drained soil that is rich in organic matter. You can set out transplants in either spring or fall. Heliopsis tolerates drought, but to keep it looking its best you should water weekly during summer dry spells. If you keep cutting off the old flowers, the plant will bloom until September.

The simplest way to propagate this perennial is to divide it in early spring. Divide plants every two to three years, or when they begin to produce fewer flowers. You can also start seeds indoors in late winter and then transplant the seedlings outdoors in spring. Seed from reputable mail-order sources will nearly always produce the desired selection, while seed saved from hybrid plants in your garden may produce seedlings that revert to the wild type.

Many heliopsis hybrids mix handsomely with asters, purple coneflowers, and phlox.

Sunflower heliopsis is named for its sunflower-like blooms that open in late summer.

Hellebore

Christmas rose, a white species of hellebore, faces upward in defiance of winter's chill.

Although attractive year-round, hellebores are at their best in winter and early spring. Beginning in mid- to late winter, these graceful, shade-loving perennials unfurl flowers in pearly shades of white, rose, burgundy, or green against the backdrop of their bold evergreen foliage. Up close, you can lift a blossom and behold its fine detail. The durable flowers remain intact for three to four months, adding color and consistency to a perennial bed or border, while the foliage serves as a dependable evergreen ground cover for shady beds throughout the year.

In the Landscape

Because of their handsome and long-lasting evergreen foliage, hellebores are grown for a ground cover as well as for their blooms. Although there are several species, all of them work well planted together. In spring, hellebores will produce numerous seedlings, so a planting will naturalize to cover a hillside or edge a shady path. Plant hellebores in the shade among ferns for contrast. They also work in a mixed border, or near a permanent feature, such as a statue or a fountain.

The apple green bells of bearsfoot hellebores are clustered on upright stems, making a striking statement in winter and early spring.

Other good summer companions for hellebores include caladiums and deciduous ferns. A small clump of hellebores will serve as a textural accent to such stalwarts of the winter garden as Christmas fern, autumn fern, rhododendron, and boxwood. If the leaves should emerge from winter looking ragged, cut

White caladiums brighten a mass of evergreen Lenten rose foliage in the summer.

AT A GLANCE
❖
HELLEBORE
Helleborus species

Features: evergreen foliage, winter blooms

Colors: white, rose, burgundy

Height: 8 to 14 inches

Light: shade

Soil: fertile, moist, well drained

Water: medium

Pests: none specific

Native: no

Range: Zones 3 to 8

Remarks: ideal plant for shade gardens

away the damaged foliage when the flowers appear. The new spring growth will shoot up just in time to conceal the faded flower. Do not remove the flowers or you will not have seedlings.

Different Species

Four species of hellebores are popular in the garden. Although collectively called hellebores, the individual species have varied common names.

True to its name, Lenten rose *(Helleborus orientalis)* blooms during the Lenten season, from January through April and even into May in the middle South. This hardy perennial is the easiest hellebore to grow in most of the South. Its nodding flowers vary in color from cream to burgundy. Some flowers sport their color in charming rosy freckles around the yellow center. You will enjoy the flowers even more if they are planted along a ledge or a winding uphill path where you can see into the blooms.

Christmas rose *(Helleborus niger)* blooms about the same time as Lenten rose, sometimes later, and is more difficult to grow. Its snowy white flowers are held erect, resembling old-fashioned, single-form roses. It grows best in the middle and upper South.

The leathery foliage of bearsfoot hellebore *(Helleborus foetidus)* resembles a bear's clawed foot and gives this herbaceous evergreen its common name. Native to western Europe, bearsfoot hellebore grows about 1 foot tall. In January and February, pendulous blossoms, resembling bell clappers, cluster atop the foliage. The flowers are apple green with a thin, rosy edge. The two-tone effect of flowers and foliage is sure to attract attention in the winter garden. After the seed matures, the flower stalks turn brown and you can cut them off. The offspring of bearsfoot hellebore are plentiful but not numerous enough to become a problem.

Although many people consider it deciduous, green hellebore *(Helleborus viridis)* is evergreen. By January, the leaves are ragged and gardeners may choose to cut them away or leave the old foliage to disintegrate as new leaves appear in late winter or early spring. The seedlings of green hellebore may be susceptible to drought, so they will need a bit more care than those of other species.

Planting and Care

Plant hellebores in the shade of pines or in a bed on the north end of your house where shade is cast all the time. Prepare your planting

Lift the nodding blossoms of Lenten rose to enjoy their rosy, freckled faces.

Sculpturally perfect blossoms of bearsfoot hellebore make it one of winter's premier perennials.

Hellebore

Green hellebore grows into an even mound of bright foliage and is therefore a superb edging plant.

bed by working in plenty of compost, leaf mold, or other organic matter. Hellebores prefer a neutral to slightly alkaline soil, so raise the pH to about 7.0 by adding lime. Once established, hellebores are practically maintenance free throughout most of the South. However, they do not grow well in the tropical regions of Florida and Texas.

Propagate hellebores by digging and transplanting seedlings. It may take three to four years for the seedlings to bloom, but you can enjoy the foliage immediately. Mature plants rarely need to be divided, but if you want to give a plant away, dig in fall and remember that the disturbed plant may not flower the following spring.

Lenten rose is quite effective when grown in a mass. This planting is brightened by the faces of early daffodils.

Hosta

These hostas sport blue and variegated foliage—a departure from common green.

Hostas are some of the most durable, long-lived, and outstanding performers for shade gardens, and there is amazing diversity within the group. Depending on the type, hostas grow from 3 inches to 4 feet in height, and their foliage color ranges from waxy blue to bright chartreuse. In bloom, they feature slender spires of white and lavender lilylike flowers, some of which are fragrant.

Hostas will live for decades without needing to be divided. However, they do not do well in the tropical regions of Florida and Texas.

In the Landscape

Use hostas as accents, in borders, in small mass plantings, or as a ground cover. They are also good companions for ferns, caladiums, coleus, and impatiens—other summer shade lovers. When planted so that the different sizes and colors form a leafy patchwork, they can create an intriguing interplay of light and texture. Hostas with bright gold or chartreuse foliage shine like a light when contrasted with deep green shades usually found in a garden. Variegated types enliven green or blue foliage with rims and swirls of gold, cream, or white. By themselves, single large hostas make striking specimen plants.

Species and Selections

The first thing to consider when choosing a hosta is leaf color. Plants can be divided into categories based on foliage color: blue, green, yellow, and variegated.

Blue hostas actually have green leaves, but a waxy coating gives the plants a blue cast that may wear off by midsummer. Mature

---

AT A GLANCE
❖
HOSTA
Hosta species

Features: long-lived plants with lush foliage from summer to fall

Colors: green, blue-green, yellow, and variegated

Height: 3 inches to 4 feet

Light: light shade

Soil: rich, well drained

Water: medium to high

Pests: slugs, snails

Native: no

Range: Zones 3 to 8

Remarks: mixes well with ferns for shade

Hosta

Blue hostas attract attention when grown in a large clump.

Royal Standard is grown for its showy, fragrant white flowers as well as for its green foliage.

plants in the upper South bear leaves as large as a serving platter. A clump of *Hosta sieboldiana* Elegans or Ryan's Big One may grow to 3½ feet tall and 4 to 6 feet wide. These plants do not get this large in the lower South because the weather is too hot. However, they will reach 2 feet in height with an equal or greater spread. These are slow growers; it takes them 5 years or more to reach full size. Other good blues are Blue Wedgwood, Blue Skies, and Halcyon.

Green hostas may not be as interesting as those with gold, blue, or variegated leaves, but you should not discount them. Green selections still serve as excellent background plantings and ground covers, where some of the more colorful types would be too vivid. In addition, the hostas with the most fragrant blossoms have green leaves; Royal Standard, Honey Bells, and *Hosta plantaginea* have large, white, fragrant blossoms.

Variegated hostas include some of the old-fashioned hostas you see planted in established neighborhoods. A popular choice is *Hosta undulata* Albomarginata, a green plant with white margins. It is inexpensive and rugged. Among the newer choices is Golden Tiara, with green leaves and gold borders. It forms a compact mound of heart-shaped foliage and sends up lavender blossoms in early summer. Kabitan, a dwarf with straplike leaves, stays less than 8 inches tall, making it a good choice for an edging. If you are looking for a very small hosta, try *Hosta gracillima* Variegated. Instead of forming

Variegated hostas brighten shady walks.

Albomarginata is one of the most popular hostas for ground cover. It is inexpensive and spreads rapidly.

clumps, it spreads by **stolons,** or creeping stems, and is no more than 3 inches tall. Frances Williams is one of the country's most popular hostas, growing 2 to 3 feet tall with large, blue leaves that have a gold outline. This selection does not like the sun; the direct sun often burns its gold borders, especially when the tender new leaves appear before the shading trees sprout leaves in spring.

Yellow hostas draw the most attention with unusual gold-to-chartreuse shades; they are not always easy to use. However, in the right place, they will provide brilliance unmatched by other plants. Use the yellow hue to its best advantage by placing it in contrast with deeply colored backgrounds. One of the grandest, Sum and Substance, bears 1- to 2-foot leaves on 3- to 4-foot plants. Other good yellows are Golden Prayers, with heart-shaped, puckered leaves, and August Moon, whose mature leaves are large like Sum and Substance but their surface has a quilted texture.

Planting and Care

Hostas do well in the shade but like a little bit of sun. The best sites receive morning sun or light dappled by trees. Plant hostas in a well-drained spot with good soil to which organic matter has been added.

Hostas need plenty of water. Their large leaves absorb moisture, so keep plants well watered during dry weather.

Before you buy, it is also wise to check with the garden center or a local hosta enthusiast about any peculiarities regarding care. Many hostas cost as much as a small tree or shrub, so do get advice before purchasing a plant.

Troubleshooting

Be prepared to fight slugs and snails. See page 125 for more about these pests.

Yellow-leafed August Moon hostas punctuate a walkway lined with carpet bugleweed.

Iris

The upright flowers and foliage of bearded iris contrast nicely with the rounded shapes of boxwood and the prostrate form of dianthus.

Of all the perennials, iris may be the most universally grown. In this large and varied group you will find types for hot, dry sites, shady bogs, the dry shade under trees, a cutting garden, or just for a flowering accent. Iris come in several shapes and sizes and, if chosen carefully, can offer blooms in three seasons. Many are maintenance free, though some require pampering, but all produce classic flowers and handsome foliage that may be as striking as the blooms themselves.

Bearded Iris

In mid- to late spring, bearded iris produce huge blooms whose lower petals sport a goatee of fuzzy hairs. Although the flowers come in just about every color, bearded iris are prized as much for their foliage as for their blooms. Long after the flowers fade, 8- to 24-inch-tall vertical leaves offer striking form to complement horizontal, creeping plants, such as creeping thyme and dianthus, or the more rounded form of peonies.

In the Landscape

Bearded iris are often planted in single-file borders or in beds by themselves; when these gorgeous flowers are not in bloom, you are left with formal plantings of green, spiky foliage. Instead, you can incorporate iris into beds and borders with other sun-loving flowers, such as blue phlox, pansies, peonies, candytuft, artemisia, or yarrow. Some iris rebloom again in the fall; yellow and wine-colored rebloomers make good companions for fall-blooming perennials and foliage plants.

Different Selections

Newer selections of bearded iris have been bred for larger, more abundant flowers in many exotic colors. They are wonderful when cut, winning ribbons at flower shows, but they also demand more attention than some of the tougher types. For landscaping, plant tried-and-true iris, such as Arctic Fury (white), Beverly Sills (coral pink), Blue Sapphire, Carolina Gold, Debbie Rairdon (white and creamy yellow), Mary Frances (light orchid-blue), Stepping Out (purple and white), and Vanity (pink).

Iris breeders have developed a reblooming iris that will bloom again in fall. These perennials come in all of the colors of regular iris and in tall, intermediate, and dwarf sizes. A few selections are Pink Attraction, I Do (white), Buckwheat (yellow), Violet Returns, and Plum Wine. But to get a fall show as spectacular as the one in spring, you must keep the plants growing vigorously throughout summer and prevent them from going dormant. Water regularly and give them plenty of food. Sprinkle a tablespoon of slow-release fertilizer around the base of each plant in spring, just after the last blossoms fade, and repeat in midsummer.

Planting and Care

Bearded iris demand full sun and good drainage. Growing from fleshy rhizomes, these iris are surprisingly drought tolerant, requiring water only when planted and in the spring. They prefer dry soil in summer and a cool winter, thus they do not thrive in the coastal South.

Plant bearded iris in late winter, summer, or fall. Work compost, shredded leaves, or other organic matter into the soil. Plant rhizomes a foot apart, taking care not to bury them completely. Do not cover the rhizomes with mulch; mulch between the iris, leaving the tops of the rhizomes to bake in the sun. Divide iris in the fall when the rhizomes become hunched and crowded. Lift the rhizomes from the ground with a turning fork and cut away the oldest and leave the younger ones. Each remaining section should have feeder roots and a fan of leaves.

Troubleshooting

If you find leaves turning yellow, dripping sap, and dying, the culprit may be an iris borer, a caterpillar that burrows through the rhizomes. Leaves of infected plants look ragged near the base where the caterpillar first begins chewing. Discourage the pest in late summer and fall by cleaning up any old, brown foliage where a moth may lay eggs to overwinter. In spring, you can spray the lower half of the plants with an approved insecticide to kill the emerging larvae.

A fuzzy "beard" on each lower petal gives bearded iris its name.

Japanese roof iris' spikes of blue blooms stand 10 to 12 inches tall.

Japanese Roof Iris

Japanese roof iris gets its name from the Japanese superstition that growing it at the edges of a thatched roof brings good luck. In early spring, the plants send up 10- to 12-inch-tall spikes of lilac-blue or white blossoms with petals that are spread apart like an open-faced sandwich. When not in bloom, the arching fans of handsome light green evergreen leaves make an elegant ground cover.

In the Landscape

Perfect for naturalizing in sun or partial shade, Japanese roof iris multiply freely to form a large mass in a few years. They are good companions for naturalizing with daffodils in a shady woodland garden, or you may also use them in clumps in a sunny bed. Combine them with hellebores, daffodils, and daylilies. Unlike the more rigid leaves of bearded iris, Japanese roof iris foliage is a bit floppy, giving a softening effect to a bed or a ground cover.

Planting and Care

Japanese roof iris bloom best in full sun although they will take some shade. They also need moist but well-drained soil. You can increase the size of your planting quickly by letting spent flowers form seedpods; in midsummer when the pods turn brown, open the pods, gather the seed, and sow it directly into the garden, about ¼ inch deep. Seedlings will emerge in thick stands within two months. When the seedlings reach 2 to 3 inches tall, separate and transplant them to empty spots in the garden, spacing them about a foot apart.

Japanese roof iris propagate easily enough by division, but you will get better plants and more of them by gathering and sowing seed.

Planted above a stacked stone wall, this mass of white Japanese roof iris offers pristine white blooms atop elegant green foliage.

Louisiana Iris

Native to Louisiana's wild wetlands, this iris enjoys moist soil conditions and is popular for low, wet areas and the edges of ponds. However, they will grow almost anywhere, from soggy muck to an ordinary flower bed. Each stalk flowers first at the top, then at the bottom, followed by two to three buds in the middle. Many bloom in early spring, but late-blooming hybrids open in mid- to late spring with the first daylilies. Louisiana iris make superb cut flowers.

The leaves, which are narrow and upright, grow 3 to 4 feet tall; in the North they are killed to the ground by a hard freeze. In warmer areas of the South, however, the leaves are evergreen and actually grow fastest in winter.

In the Landscape

Louisiana iris are popular in pots submerged in a water feature, planted in flower beds to add color and vertical foliage, or placed along the edge of a stream or pond. Wherever they grow, Louisiana iris are instantly recognized by their unique foliage and thin flower stems that may flop over after a heavy rain.

Different Species

Because many hybrids have been bred over the years from such parent plants as leafy blue flag *(Iris brevicaulis)*, there are many selections of Louisiana iris that are cold hardy enough for Zone 4. They represent a spectacular color range, perhaps the widest of any group of iris, including violet, blue, purple, pink, white, magenta, red, and orange. The best way to get a selection suited to your area is to check locally. Be aware that many of the selections may not be sold by any name other than Louisiana iris.

Flag iris *(Iris pseudacorus)* is a dependable, tall, narrow-leafed species grown mostly around water, either submerged in a pot or at the edge of a pond or stream. However, it will also grow well in garden beds provided it is watered during periods of drought. The plants reach 2 to 3 feet tall and bear yellow blooms in early summer. It is hardy from Zones 5 to 9.

Siberian iris *(Iris siberica)* is another excellent choice for wet sites. This iris is so versatile that it will thrive in a pot, in water, or in the narrow strip between a street and sidewalk. Native to moist meadows, Siberian iris can be planted nearly anywhere, in full sun or partial shade. The foliage is narrow and will vary from 1 to 3 feet in

Louisiana iris punctuate the landscape with their sharp vertical form.

AT A GLANCE

LOUISIANA IRIS
Iris Louisiana hybrids

Features: exotic flowers with green, reedlike foliage

Colors: magenta, blue, white, red, pink, orange, violet, purple

Height: 3 to 4 feet

Light: full sun

Soil: rich, moist, acid

Water: medium to high

Pests: none specific

Native: yes

Range: Zones 3 to 10

Remarks: great for ponds and water features

Known for their vast color range, Louisiana iris are among the most hybridized of the iris family.

height, depending on the amount of water the plant receives. Selections bear flowers in deep purple, various shades of blue, and white. Siberian iris grows in Zones 3 to 9.

Planting and Care

Louisiana iris need at least six hours of sun a day. (In hot, dry climates, give them afternoon shade.) Before planting, loosen the soil to a depth of at least a foot and work in plenty of organic matter. These plants prefer acid soil.

The best time to plant is in late summer or early fall when plants are dormant. Promptly unwrap the roots of plants that arrive in the mail and store them in water until you are ready to plant. Set these rhizomes at or slightly below the soil surface, spacing them at least a foot apart. If you plant in spring, keep them well watered. For a waterside planting, do not plant the rhizomes directly in the water. Instead, place them at the water's edge. Iris planted on land need no more moisture than other perennials. But extra water in spring and fall results in better bloom.

Dwarf Crested Iris

These dainty native iris *(Iris cristata)* grow only 4 to 6 inches tall to carpet the ground in a mass of blue and yellow early-spring blossoms. One of the most dependable wildflowers for shade, dwarf crested iris will spread to form large masses when left alone. The blooms are only an inch wide. The foliage is flat and straplike, appearing in early spring before the blossoms; in fall it disappears.

In the Landscape

Dwarf crested iris grows best in a wooded setting where it can naturalize. If possible, plant these iris so you can enjoy them from a terrace or a window. Or let them spread along a shady walkway or driveway. When grown in a bed, they must be planted in masses away from heavy shade and competing roots of taller plants. Suitable companions include such perennials as wild columbine and wild ginger. Maidenhair fern will also work well with dwarf crested iris, provided the soil does not get too dry for the fern.

Different Selections

Most dwarf crested iris are sold under that name. However, you may find a white variety, Alba, which is not quite as vigorous as the blue.

Planting and Care

Once established, dwarf crested iris will take care of itself, often tolerating the dry conditions under large shade trees. However, the plants will bloom best if they receive some sunlight and are well watered during dry periods.

Plant in late winter or early spring in well-drained soil. Set rhizomes ½ to 1 inch deep. Each rhizome will produce 3 to 4 new roots every year. Once settled in the home garden, dwarf crested iris spreads quickly by long, thin rhizomes that creep just below the soil surface or at ground level.

You can start new plantings or dig plants to give away by separating established clumps. Dig in fall or late winter.

Louisiana iris are well adapted to boggy conditions.

Lamb's-ear

Even in the summer, lamb's-ears look cool and refreshing, as if lightly frosted.

One look at the floppy, soft, woolly leaves will tell you how lamb's-ear gets its name. However, the appeal of lamb's-ear goes far beyond softness. The silvery-gray foliage is as elegant as it is interesting. The plant's mound of leaves grows 6 to 12 inches tall and stands in contrast to the green foliage or flower colors of adjacent plantings. And the 4- to 6-inch-long leaves provide a coarse, textural break as well.

In the Landscape

Although it is attractive when used alone, the greatest asset of lamb's-ear is its capacity to bring out the colors of surrounding flowers and foliage. Finer leafed companion plants include the perennial dianthus and catmint, or the annual Madagascar periwinkle and narrowleaf zinnia. It is also handsome at the base of old-fashioned pink roses, such as the Fairy rose.

While the leaves of lamb's-ears are attractive all season long, the early summer flower stalks cause the plant to stretch, destroying its ground-cover effect. The leafy mat sprouts 12- to 18-inch spikes of purplish-pink flowers. Pinch off the flower stalks as they begin to shoot upward or plant the selection Silver Carpet, which never blooms. Use the bloom stalks in flower arrangements.

Different Selections

Usually sold simply as lamb's-ear, this plant is not often found in a wide variety of selections at garden centers. However, if you are lucky, you may find a few that are particularly outstanding. Silver Carpet is nice because it does not produce the tall bloom spikes. Helen von Stein is prized for its large leaves and tolerance of hot, humid conditions.

Planting and Care

Put lamb's-ears near the front of a bed where they will not be hidden by taller plants. Best planted in spring, they will grow together during their first season. Although they will tolerate partial shade, the more sun they receive, the stronger they will be. They do need excellent drainage.

To keep a clump of lamb's-ears looking fresh, prune plants in late winter. The only regular maintenance required is trimming back the edges of the plants, to help keep the center of the plant full, and removing decayed leaves, which are unsightly and may encourage

The purplish-pink spikes bloom in early summer.

rot. Also remove flower stalks as they appear or as the flowers fade, depending on your preference.

Lamb's-ears spread so fast that you will probably need to divide them in spring or fall every two to three years. As a plant ages, new growth comes out from the tips of the stems while the foliage dies out in the center. Divide the plants by digging them up and separating the healthy stems. Even if these do not have many roots, place the stems on their sides and cover lightly with soil. Keep them moist, but not too wet.

Lamb's-ears are cold hardy in the South, but gardeners in Florida and along the Gulf Coast may have problems in summer as constant heat and humidity can damage the plants, even in well-drained, sandy soil. When watering, try to keep moisture off the leaves because they tend to trap humidity, thereby promoting leaf rot. Avoid using a sprinkler, and water plants in the morning so that they have time to dry out before nightfall.

Best planted near the front of a border, lamb's-ears spread into a leafy mat that grows taller just before the plant blooms.

Moss Verbena

Blooming all summer and fall, moss verbena stops flowering only at frost.

Fans of roadside flowers may recognize moss verbena as the low-growing wildflower that produces a carpet of purple flowers all summer. Even in hot, dry, windswept conditions, it just keeps on blooming, which is why many gardeners use it as a mainstay of summer beds, border edgings, and rock gardens. Unlike annual verbena, moss verbena is resistant to diseases and insects, and it is also a better garden performer.

A South American native, moss verbena is naturalized in the lower and coastal South, where it grows as a perennial. It can be grown as an annual by gardeners in cool areas, and it is worth replanting every spring. Similar in color and habit to moss pink *(Phlox subulata),* moss verbena has dark, glossy foliage that grows unblemished in a lacy, green mat in full sun. Although some of this foliage remains green through winter, severe freezes will kill most of the top growth. However, new leaves sprout with the warming weather, and the plant is in bloom by May in the middle South. But spring is just the beginning for moss verbena, whose display lasts until frost, especially if you trim back the old, spent blooms several times during the season.

In the Landscape

Moss verbena's lavender-purple blooms make an excellent combination with pale yellow flowers, such as Moonbeam coreopsis. Some gardeners prefer the white-flowered moss verbena selection called Alba, or a mix of the two.

An ideal plant for the front of a sunny flower border, moss verbena can be planted with spring bulbs. Coming into bloom about the time the bulb foliage fades, it will carry the show for the rest of the season. Use moss verbena as a ground cover on gentle slopes, in rocky soil, and in areas prone to drought. It is also a good choice for the edge of a driveway or even among the pebbles of a gravel parking court or walkway.

Because it may reseed or spread by rooting stems, you will find moss verbena will naturalize in sunny gardens much as it does along roadsides. Take advantage of this, especially on large properties.

Planting and Care

Choose a sunny, well-drained location, and moss verbena will thrive. Although it becomes leggy and thin without enough light, the only sure way to kill it is to plant it in soggy soil. When moss verbena starts looking bedraggled in midsummer, trim it back to 3 to 4 inches and it will rebound crisp and pretty. In areas where it is not perennial, you may see it reappear from seed the next spring.

Moss verbena spreads by layering; that is, the stems root as they creep across the soil. A planting of perennial moss verbena will undoubtedly get larger.

Moss verbena is the perfect summer edging plant for a walkway, lining it with a mat of color.

Peony

Peonies are quite handsome, especially in flower arrangements.

For spontaneity, exuberance, and beauty, few perennials can surpass peonies. Each spring, this hardy perennial comes up from just a few roots to become a sturdy, shrublike plant that is covered with dense, leathery foliage and dozens of exquisite flowers. Once planted, a peony often lives for decades. Peonies are delightful cut flowers in spring arrangements.

In the Landscape

Because of their large blossoms, peonies are at their best when grown in large groups to create a mass of color. They are also effective in a perennial border, especially when contrasted with such strongly vertical plants as bearded iris and poppies.

After they bloom, these fine, dense plants serve as a background for later perennials that grow no taller than 2 to 3 feet, such as coreopsis and asters.

Species and Selections

Peonies must have some cold weather, but there are many selections that perform beautifully as far south as Zone 7 and the northern half of Zone 8. The key is choosing a selection that blooms early. (See chart on opposite page.)

The single-flowered Japanese peonies bloom reliably. Semidouble or double forms are more likely to become waterlogged and attract disease. But if you want a double-flowered peony, choose an early-flowering one, such as Festiva Maxima, a beautiful white that does well even in Zone 8.

Tree peony *(Peonia suffruticosa)* has a woody stem that does not die back to the ground each year. It will grow well in Zones 6 and 7 but needs protection from cold in Zone 5. Tree peonies also prefer neutral to slightly alkaline soil, so adjust the pH to 7.0 in the South. They require shade in the afternoon.

Most tree peonies grow 3 to 5 feet tall but may need pruning down to a foot high every few years to encourage new growth.

The early blooming peonies are likely to bloom at the same time as bearded iris.

Planting and Care

The best time to plant peonies is in fall, although they can also be planted in spring. While directions will tell you to plant several inches deep, in the South the red eyes (sprouts) on the root should be placed no more than ½ to 1 inch below ground level for best flowering. Peonies resent transplanting, so plant them in a spot where they will stay.

Peonies need full sun or light shade, well-drained soil, and lots of water, especially in spring. Use only low-nitrogen fertilizer in spring; overdoing it can produce too much foliage and fewer flowers. Also, stake the plants or let them grow through a wire support early in the season to bear the weight of the foliage and flowers.

SOME EARLY BLOOMING PEONIES

Selections	Flower Color	Flower Type
Charles White	White	Double
Dancing Nymph	White	Single
Edulis Superba	Pink	Double
Festiva Maxima	White/red flecks	Double
Krinkled White	White	Single
Lady Alexandra Duff	Pale pink	Semidouble
Largo	Pink	Single
Sarah Bernhardt	Pink	Double
Scarlett O'Hara	Red	Single

Be patient—blooms will be disappointing the first year but improve in succeeding seasons.

Do not remove more than two or three leaves with a stem; the plant needs its foliage for steady growth. If you need long stems with more foliage, do not cut more than half of the flowers on the plant. If you want extralarge flowers for arranging, pinch off the buds that develop along the sides of the stem as soon as they appear, allowing only the terminal bud to develop.

Troubleshooting

Thrips (thin, black insects smaller than a grain of rice) and beetles can ruin the blooms. Also, cut back the foliage each fall after the first hard freeze to prevent the spread of disease.

Tree peony is a woody plant that does not die back to the ground in winter the way other peonies do.

Single-flowered peonies are less likely to be damaged in a rainstorm than the double-flowered types.

Phlox

A delight in early spring, woodland phlox dots roadsides, meadows, and mountainsides. This native is easy to grow, offering striking lavender-blue flowers that spruce up perennial borders and bring early spring life to shady beds and wildflower gardens.

Woodland phlox will thrive throughout the South except in the southernmost areas of Florida and Texas. The blossoms are slightly fragrant and appear from early to midspring in time to mix with daffodils and other early blossoms. The blooms are about 1 inch wide and are borne in clusters atop foot-long stems. Colors range from lavender-blue to pale violet and white. The display lasts about three weeks, and then the flowers form seeds, which self-sow to thicken the planting. Leaves often turn brown shortly after the blossoms fade; new leaves appear in late summer or early fall.

In the Landscape

Woodland phlox has a low, mat-forming habit, making it an excellent woodland ground cover. Combine the plant with others in rock gardens and flower borders, but do not put it in prominent spots by itself. The plant is not very attractive in late spring when the flowers go to seed or in midsummer when the foliage is brown. Consider interplanting woodland phlox with spring bulbs, such as daffodils or tulips, or mix it with hardy ferns to camouflage it during these times.

The blue shades of woodland phlox are strong enough to hold their own among bolder colors. This plant combines well with bright hyacinths, bearded iris, and yellow pansies or primroses.

In a more formal, cultivated border, woodland phlox makes a good companion to bulbs.

Woodland phlox is perfect for lining a shady walk.

AT A GLANCE

WOODLAND PHLOX
Phlox divaricata

Features: early spring blooms
Colors: blue, violet, white
Height: 12 to 15 inches
Light: partial shade
Soil: moist, rich
Water: medium
Pests: powdery mildew if stressed by drought
Native: yes
Range: Zones 5 to 9
Remarks: reseeds, requires little care

Fuller's White offers color variation in the garden.

Species and Selections

Woodland phlox comes in many shades of blue, from true blue to nearly pink. It also comes in white. Many of the wild forms have the slightest hint of pink, although there are actually no true pink selections. Plants that are raised from the seed of native species may vary in color. Named selections are propagated from cuttings and should be consistent in color. Dirgo Ice is a pale lavender-blue form about 8 to 12 inches tall. Fuller's White is more tolerant of sun than most other selections; it also blooms a bit longer, often lasting over a month. Louisiana Blue is an early-flowering purplish-blue phlox.

For larger flowers, try Laphamii *(Phlox divaricata* Laphamii*)*, a subspecies with blue-violet flowers that lacks the characteristic notch on each petal. Laphamii tolerates more sun than other selections. Chattahoochee is a hybrid of Laphamii and another native, Downy phlox *(Phlox pilosa)*. It has a magenta eye in the center of each blue flower, and it stays in bloom longer than wild species of woodland phlox—often over a month. Chattahoochee tolerates full sun and sandy soil. It grows in Zones 5 to 9 and is not quite as hardy as woodland phlox.

Downy phlox blooms later than woodland phlox, mixing well with early roses or the light green of newly emerged ferns. Ozarkana is a pink selection that tolerates sun as well as partial shade. It grows in the range of woodland phlox.

Creeping phlox *(Phlox stolonifera)* is not quite as showy or vigorous as woodland phlox. However, it tolerates even deeper shade, making it a good choice for heavily wooded lots. This native grows from Zones 2 to 8 and is quite hardy.

Planting and Care

The best time to plant is in fall so the plants can become established before they bloom in early spring. However, you may also plant in spring when they are likely to appear in full bloom in garden centers.

Growing wild from Canada to north Florida and west to Texas, woodland phlox also easily adapts to garden conditions. It prefers dappled sunlight in spring and shade in summer, conditions found under deciduous trees. If the soil is not fairly rich, amend it before planting with generous amounts of organic matter, such as compost, manure, or sphagnum peat moss. Roots are shallow, so mulch with more organic matter to help conserve moisture.

Woodland phlox usually sur-vives summer drought—the plants are dormant at that time—but avoid open sites as the summer sun is too harsh and bakes the soil. Occasionally you may see powdery mildew on the leaves, especially on plants that have been stressed dur-ing a dry winter, but the plants recover on their own.

Starting from Seed

If left alone, woodland phlox will reseed and multiply. Each plant will also spread gradually to form a clump, so you can increase plant-ings by dividing clumps every third year in fall or spring. In fact, this is the best way to propagate hybrids, which do not come true from seed. Divide older plantings to renew them in spring just after they bloom or in the fall.

Another easy way to propa-gate woodland phlox is by ground layering. Bend a piece of stem to the ground, place a handful of soil on top, and weight the stem down with a stone or a brick. Rooting will be complete in about two weeks. You may then transfer the rooted layers to their new locations.

As its name implies, woodland phlox is at home in a wooded setting where it can reseed and spread as a ground cover.

Primrose

In spring, the Japanese primrose blooms along tall flower stalks.

With plant heights that rise and fall like musical notes, Japanese primrose combines the colorful impact of phlox with the architectural beauty of hosta. It is also one of the easiest primroses to grow, provided it has a steady supply of water.

This plant is a boon to gardeners for its spring blooms in shady, boggy sites, often the death of many well-known perennials. From a tuft of bright green, spinachlike leaves, it produces whorled tiers of blooms up to 2 feet tall in vivid colors ranging from white to pink to red to purple. When not in bloom, the foliage remains a handsome rosette of 6- to 12-inch-long leaves.

In the Landscape

The banks of a stream or a pond are good sites for Japanese primrose, which needs consistent moisture. It is also an excellent choice for use around birdbaths and other water features. Mass groups of a single color in the moist shade along the banks of a wooded stream, or blend purples, whites, and pinks for a more dazzling look. Also try Japanese primrose with other moisture and shade-loving plants, such as hostas, Virginia bluebells, or ferns.

Different Selections

Several garden catalogs offer mixtures of pink, rose, purple, and white, selections that return from seed in a variety of hues. For solid colors, try Miller's Crimson or Postford White (white with a yellow eye). Miller's Crimson will come back a true color from seed. Cowslip primrose, *Primula veris*, is a related plant with smaller yellow flowers. Cowslip is better adapted to garden conditions in shady beds and will grow well throughout the middle South.

Planting and Care

The soil should be acid and evenly moist, but not soggy, and should contain plenty of organic matter. If the soil is too wet, the plant may

AT A GLANCE
❖
JAPANESE PRIMROSE
Primula japonica

Features: spectacular spring blooms on candelabra-like stems

Colors: white, pink, red, purple

Height: 1 to 2 feet, in bloom

Light: light shade

Soil: moist, acid, rich

Water: high

Pests: none specific

Native: no

Range: Zones 5 to 8

Remarks: likes boggy conditions; easy to grow

be heaved out of the ground in winter, particularly in the upper South. If it is too dry, it may die shortly after blooming and setting seed. If the soil is consistently moist, plants should thrive and spread by new seedlings each year. Japanese primroses also demand shade (with no more than one hour of direct morning sun). High shade from tall hardwoods or pines works well. While individual plants live only a few years, you will never miss them because new seedlings take their place.

To establish a new planting, set out transplants in the spring or start plants from seed. The time to sow outside is when the seeds ripen—late summer to early fall. Simply scatter the seed over bare soil where you want seedlings to sprout.

Japanese primroses thrive in moist, acid soil and light shade, lending sensational color to the banks of a pond when planted in masses.

Soft shades of Japanese primrose create a light, lacy effect in the spring garden.

Salvia

Anise sage has some of the largest blooms of any salvia. Its azure flowers can be 2 inches long.

Most summer flowers are past their prime in fall. Not so with perennial salvias, which have a way of saving the day. Fall is when many of them come into their full glory, with brilliant spikes of blue, purple, or red flowers.

While many salvias are reliably hardy through Zone 7, a few can be considered perennial only from Zone 8 southward. Yet salvias are so fast growing and provide so much color for so little effort that you will want to grow them even if they are only annual in your garden.

You have probably used the popular annual salvia (*Salvia splendens,* or scarlet sage) as a bedding plant for summer color, and you may have grown culinary sage (*Salvia officinalis*) in your herb garden. These are two relatives of perennial flowering salvias and are commonly referred to as sage.

At a Glance
❖
SALVIA
Salvia species

Features: natural, shrublike plants; dramatic color

Colors: blue, purple, red, rose, white

Height: 1 to 6 feet

Light: full sun to partial shade

Soil: average, well drained

Water: medium

Pests: whiteflies

Native: some

Range: Zones 2 to 10

Remarks: easy to grow, blooms for a long time

In the Landscape

Some salvias are shrublike and are therefore impressive as specimens or grouped in borders. Because of this, they make good back-of-the-border plants, and may be planted along fences and in herb gardens. For contrast, pair blue and purple salvias with strong yellow flowers, such as coneflowers, sunflowers, mums, or marigolds. Or group several blue and white salvias together for a clean, natural effect; add pink yarrow, lamb's-ear, or Shasta daisies for a cottage touch. Perennial salvias can be the primary feature of the landscape during the growing season, adding low-maintenance color for up to six months. Smaller selections add visual impact in containers.

A fall salvia, Mexican bush sage mixes well with yellow swamp sunflowers and the burgundy foliage of Red Shield hibiscus.

Species and Selections

Mexican bush sage or velvet sage *(Salvia leucantha)* is a fall salvia with thin gray-green leaves and abundant fuzzy purple flowers atop 15- to 20-inch spikes. It blooms from late summer to the first frost on plants that grow 3 to 4 feet tall, sometimes taller in warm areas. Emerald is a selection with purple spikes and white centers; All Purple has entirely purple flowers. Mexican bush sage is not perennial north of Zone 8 but will reach its full size even if grown as an annual. A single-stemmed transplant set in the garden in late spring will reward you with a vase-shaped plant that will be 4 feet tall and equally wide by the time it blooms in September. Mexican bush sage is an unusually pretty cut flower; hang bouquets upside down in a breezeway to dry them to perfection.

Anise sage *(Salvia guaranitica),* another late bloomer, boasts the largest flowers of all salvias and has foliage with a faint spicy scent. Wisps of 1½- to 2-inch-long bluish-purple flowers appear on the 3-foot plants all summer. One selection, Late Blooming Giant, reaches 9 or 10 feet. It is best used as an annual in all but the lower and coastal South, planted in well-drained soil in light shade. A native of South America, this salvia is a favorite of hummingbirds and works well in wildflower and butterfly gardens. Argentine Skies has blue flowers.

Autumn sage *(Salvia greggii)* is native to Texas. It is perennial in the lower and coastal South, where it blooms generously from spring until frost (despite its name). It puts on an equally impressive show as an annual farther north. Autumn sage boasts dozens of sparkling blooms in magenta, red, coral, or white. Because it is open in form, this salvia

Autumn sage is brilliant in fall with magenta, white, or pale red flowers.

should be paired with solid-colored, fuller flowers, such as Queen Anne's lace or white daisies. Autumn sage is drought tolerant and does not mind alkaline soil or heavy soil, even red clay. Give it full or partial shade.

Mealycup sage *(Salvia farinacea)* is one of the best known perennial salvias and is the most readily available. It is native to Texas and other parts of the Southwest. Although mealycup sage is neither dependably perennial nor long-lived, gardeners who grow it as an annual come to rely on its continous flowers from early summer until frost. Victoria is one of the hardiest selections, with rich, deep blue flowers. The plants will grow about 18 inches tall and bloom all summer long. Blue Bedder is less hardy; it has light blue flowers and may reach 24 inches tall. White Porcelain is a selection with white blooms that grows about 15 inches tall. Prune this salvia if it begins to look leggy (usually in August). With extra watering, it will come back with a passion in fall. It also does double duty as a cut flower—fresh or dried.

Pineapple sage offers fragrant foliage topped by the truest red flowers of fall.

Pineapple sage *(Salvia elegans)* hails from Mexico and is appreciated for its delicate red flowers and the fruity fragrance of its leaves, which can be used fresh or dried in cakes, teas, and herbal seasonings. This plant is sometimes labeled *Salvia rutilans.* Like Mexican bush sage, this salvia waits until fall to yield a floral display, but it provides a grand finale to summer. It is not always cold hardy north of Zone 9.

Forsythia salvia *(Salvia madrensis)* is an unusual yellow-flowered species. It is a good companion to fall-blooming perennials as its blooms do not open until October.

Hybrid salvias are also available for the perennial garden. Indigo Spires has rich purple flowers that stand above leafy green foliage. Plants grow 3 to 6 feet tall; the flower stalks become longer (18 to 20 inches) and deeper in color in fall. This is a good salvia for beginners as it has many uses, performs well, and can be mixed with other blooms. It is one of the hardiest salvias, growing in Zones 3 to 8. East Friesland is another popular hybrid with deep purple blooms; it only grows about 18 inches tall. May Night is a similar selection but is a bit less tolerant of hot, humid weather.

Planting and Care

Good drainage is a must for growing salvias—they will rot in soggy soil. However, they like plenty of water during summer, especially in August. Many salvias are drought tolerant, but they all need ample water to help fuel rapid growth and high performance. Most need full sun (at least six hours) for best blooming.

Tall plants may require staking, although pinching back outer branches helps support the inner ones. Pairing tall salvias with shorter, shrubbier plants also provides support. Cut back salvias after they freeze and mulch them for protection against winter cold. Prune Mexican bush sage in early summer to keep it compact.

To propagate, divide clumps in spring or fall. For tender perennials, take 4- to 6-inch cuttings, remove the flower stalks, and set them in containers filled with moist sand; overwinter them indoors, beside a basement window or in a greenhouse or cold frame.

Troubleshooting

Pests and disease problems are minimal, although whiteflies can sometimes bother salvia. See page 125 for more about whiteflies.

The flowering stalks of Indigo Spires grow longer and more intensely colored as fall progresses.

Sedum

Showy sedum is a natural companion to arching ornamental grasses.

Showy sedum is one of the most rugged, durable perennials available. This plant is tailor-made for the gardener whose intentions are greater than his time. As long as they get plenty of light, sedums rarely disappoint, blooming in spite of forgotten waterings and a complete lack of plant food.

This late bloomer emerges in spring with succulent rosettes of leaves that grow into lush mounds of gray-green foliage. By mid-summer, flower buds take shape, looking much like beaded tufts atop the pale, smooth foliage that is similar to that of jade plant. In fall, the plants blush with color as the buds open into starlike clusters of pink, rose, crimson, or copper.

In the Landscape

Showy sedum combines nicely with shrubs and other perennials. Plant it with yellow mums, ornamental grasses, coneflowers, or asters. You may also use it to provide textural contrast for finer leafed shrubs, such as Scotch broom and cotoneaster. Mix showy sedum with plants bearing gray-green foliage, such as lamb's-ears, fernleaf yarrow, Silver Mound artemisia, or bearded iris. Because it is so drought tolerant, sedum is a choice plant to feature in an urn or other ornamental container. Place it to mark an entrance, to serve as the focal point of a path, or to add a spot of color on your terrace, deck, or patio. Thriving in full sun and clay soil, showy sedum has long been popular in rock gardens. But more gardeners are finding that sedums also make ideal perennials for borders, containers, and beds.

Different Selections

The species has soft pink blooms and is often found in old gardens. Selections display a fascinating range of shades as their flowers bloom and deepen. For example, the selection known as Autumn Joy (also called Indian Chief) blossoms from pale green buds into rich pink flowers, progresses to a salmon shade of bronze, and dries to a coppery red that persists into winter. Brilliant is a raspberry red, Meteor has deep red blooms, and Star Dust is ivory with occasional pink flowers.

AT A GLANCE
❖
SHOWY SEDUM
Sedum spectabile

Features: succulent leaves, striking flowers
Colors: pink, red, bronze
Height: 12 to 24 inches
Light: full sun to partial shade
Soil: well drained
Water: low
Pests: none specific
Native: no
Range: Zones 4 to 9
Remarks: easy to grow, long-lived

Planting and Care

Showy sedum enjoys full sun but will also grow in light shade; plants in shade may require pruning back in early summer so that they do not get too leggy. The only conditions in which showy sedum will not grow are deep shade and poor drainage.

Set out transplants or divisions in the fall or early spring. Watering is necessary only during severe drought. Do not mulch showy sedum as this promotes rot. To propagate, snip off a stem, plant it in moist soil, and watch it take root.

Its attractive, succulent mound of leaves and sculptural form make sedum an asset even when it is not in bloom.

In the fall sedum Autumn Joy slowly turns from a rich pink to a coppery red, drying on the stem. Here it grows with narrowleaf zinnia and mealy-cup sage.

121

Yarrow

Common yarrow brings deep pink to the color palette in the garden.

When yarrow blooms, it is as if the brilliant yellow sun had broken through a mask of sullen clouds. This is why many flower borders feature yarrow in late spring, summer, and occasionally in fall.

But not all yarrows are yellow. Unlike fernleaf yarrow, the yellow type, common yarrow sports flowers of pink and white. Your choice of yarrow depends on where you live and what kind of effect you want to create. Either type is a fine addition to the garden—informal, hardy, and colorful with delicate, fernlike foliage that is attractive even when the plants are not in bloom.

Yarrow is also a choice cut flower, fresh or dried. For drying and preserving, cut the flowers when they are at their peak. Use a rubber band to bind the ends of the stems together and hang the bunch upside down in a cool, dry, dark place. The flowers will be ready for arranging in three to four weeks.

Common yarrow adapts well to flower borders in hot, humid climates.

In the Landscape

Yarrow has long been a staple of herb gardens. Today it is a pleasant addition to garden borders, meadows, and mass plantings in full sun. For a mix of color and texture, try combining yarrow with pink phlox or purple-leafed plants. Other excellent companions include blue salvia and ornamental grasses.

Species and Selections

Fernleaf yarrow (*Achillea filipendulina*) makes an excellent garden plant because it stands up straight and stays where you put it. It also possesses handsome foliage that ranges from gray-green to silver. The main flush of yellow bloom appears in late May or early June and lasts about a month. Sporadic blooms then appear throughout the summer. The largest selection of fernleaf yarrow is Gold Plate, which grows 4 to 5 feet tall and nearly as wide. Its flattened clusters of tiny golden blossoms may be 6 inches across. This plant is strictly for the rear of large perennial borders. Another back-of-the-border yarrow is Parker's Variety. It grows 3 to 4 feet tall with clusters about 3 inches across. Either of these plants may require staking if planted in rich soils or overfertilized.

Common yarrow *(Achillea millefolium)* is a native of Europe that has been naturalized in this country, where it is a prolific spreader. Some consider it a weed, but if you divide it regularly in the fall and do not overfertilize, common yarrow will remain compact. It is the best yarrow for hot, humid environments. Ranging from 1 to 2 feet in height, common yarrow is covered in fine, ferny foliage and blooms from late spring to summer, and occasionally again in the fall. It is both heat and drought tolerant, hence excellent for an untended or wild area. Colors include white and rosy pink; Fire King is one of the more popular pinks on the market.

Hybrid yarrows include Coronation Gold, a hybrid between fernleaf yarrow and *Achillea clypeolata* that enjoys popularity in the South. Growing 30 to 36 inches tall, it is ideal for the middle or rear of a small flower border. Its deep golden clusters, about 3 inches across, appear atop fine, silvery-green foliage. Another popular hybrid is Moonshine. This is much lower growing than other yarrows—about 18 to 24 inches—so use it at the front of a border. Its gray foliage and canary yellow blooms are its highlights; this lighter shade is easy to blend with other flower colors. The only drawback to fernleaf yarrow and some of its hybrids is that they are not proven to be as hardy in the hot, humid coastal South.

The Pearl *(Achillea ptarmica* The Pearl) is a popular hybrid that bears clusters of white buttonlike flowers. It tends to sprawl and flop, so plant it where it can spill over an edge.

Planting and Care

Planted in the right place, yarrow is easy to grow. These perennials tolerate heat and drought but cannot stand hot, humid weather. They need bright sunshine and excellent drainage and air circulation to help protect the foliage from humid weather. Good drainage is especially important in winter, when yarrow is most susceptible to root rot. Divide every couple of years to rejuvenate and prevent overcrowding. Faithful deadheading will help keep the plant blooming all summer.

The flattened clusters of fernleaf yarrow contain hundreds of tiny blossoms.

Pests and Diseases

The following insects and diseases are common pests of the perennials in this book. To control them, you must first know your enemy; learn which plants are susceptible, what symptoms may occur, and how to combat the pests. Many techniques and pesticides are available to help you fight diseases and insect pests, but the recommendations for these products frequently change. Contact your local Extension office for information about specific pesticides.

Before using a pesticide, read the entire label. Always use pesticides strictly according to label directions. Using a pesticide in any way that is not in accordance with label recommendations is illegal.

Aphids

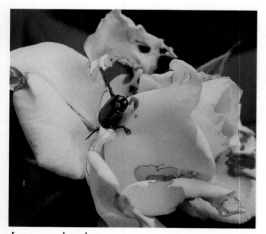

Japanese beetle

Aphids

Aphids are tiny, pear-shaped insects that are ⅛ to ¼ inch long; they are frequently green or black but may also be yellow or pink. They harm plants by sucking sap from the tender young stems and flower buds so that growth is distorted and the buds do not open. Aphids are worst in spring and fall. They will produce hundreds of offspring in a few weeks, so it is crucial to control them as soon as they appear.

Caterpillars

Caterpillars are the larvae of moths and butterflies. They generally feed on a plant's leaves without your knowledge and without causing any serious damage. These pests vary from about ½ inch to nearly 2 inches long and may be brown, green, or yellow, fuzzy or smooth, striped or solid. Control caterpillars when you first notice them because their feeding will disfigure the leaves. Spray or dust the undersides of the leaves at the first sign of their presence and keep a caterpillar dust on the foliage to prevent reinfestation.

Japanese Beetles

These ½-inch-long, metallic green-and-copper beetles will fly into your garden and are very difficult to control. Japanese beetles like to chew one plant for a short time and then fly to another plant. They usually feed in hordes, with hundreds present at a time.

Dusting foliage with a recommended pesticide helps, but you must keep the dust on new growth as it unfurls. The best way to control Japanese beetles is to kill the *grubs,* or larvae, which feed in the lawn. To do this most effectively, join forces with neighbors to treat a large area of lawn.

Powdery Mildew

Powdery mildew is a disease that looks like a white to gray mildew on the surface of the leaves. It will cause the leaves to dry and wither, thus weakening the plant.

Once the disease appears, it is difficult to control. Good air circulation is important to keep the foliage dry so that powdery mildew will not develop. If you have seen the disease in your garden before, you can generally predict its occurrence (usually in spring and fall); spray both sides of the leaves with an approved fungicide before the mildew appears. Powdery mildew is likely to affect phlox.

Powdery mildew

Slugs

Slugs are like snails without shells. They chew holes in the succulent leaves of young plants and are especially fond of hostas. Slugs feed at night, so it will be difficult to see them during the day. One sure sign of slugs is a shiny slime trail on the leaves in your garden. To see the trail clearly, hold an affected leaf in the sunlight and turn it so that the light is reflected by the slimy trail.

You can control slugs with bait, but read the label warning carefully, as most are poisonous to pets. You may trap slugs in shallow bowls of beer or beneath cantaloupe or grapefruit halves turned upside down in the garden.

Slug

Spider Mites

Spider mites are tiny spiderlike insects that collect on the underside of the leaves and on flower buds. They damage plants by sucking sap from the plants so that the leaves are deformed and the buds do not open. They are worst in spring and fall, especially during dry weather.

You may not see spider mites until their feeding begins to make the topside of the leaves look faded and mottled. Look on the undersides of leaves for the pinpoint-sized spider mites and their delicate webbing. Use a magnifying glass to be sure. To control spider mites, spray the underside of the leaves thoroughly.

Whiteflies

These white, mothlike insects are only $\frac{1}{8}$ inch long; they rest on the underside of leaves, sucking sap and leaving foliage yellowed and spotted. If you shake the plant, they will fly out, but then they will light again. To control whiteflies, spray the underside of the leaves with a recommended pesticide.

Spider mite damage

Index

Special Thanks

All-America Selections, photograph, 57

Jacqueline Giovanelli

Jennifer Greer

Southern Progress Corporation Library Staff

White Flower Farm/Michael Dodge, photograph, 60

Christina Wynn